Light Behind the Darkness

Stories of Compassion from the Holy Land

Light Behind the Darkness

Stories of Compassion from the Holy Land

RAOUF
OMAR

CLAUDE
WEIL

GENERAL STORE PUBLISHING HOUSE
499 O'Brien Road, Box 415
Renfrew, Ontario, Canada K7V 4A6
Telephone (613) 432-7697 or 1-800-465-6072
www.gsph.com

ISBN 978-1-897508-36-7

Illustrations: Raouf Omar
Design and layout: Magdalene Carson / New Leaf Publication Design
Printed by Custom Printers of Renfrew Ltd., Renfrew, Ontario
Printed and bound in Canada

Library and Archives Canada Cataloguing in Publication

Omar, Raouf, 1952-
Light behind the darkness : stories of compassion in the Holy Land / Raouf Omar, Claude Weil.

Includes bibliographical references and index.
ISBN 978-1-897508-36-7

1. Omar, Raouf, 1952-. 2. Weil, Claude, 1954-. 3. Arab-Israeli conflict--1973-1993--Personal narratives, Palestinian Arab. 4. Arab-Israeli conflict--1973-1993--Personal narratives, Jewish. I. Weil, Claude, 1954- II. Title.

DS119.7.O43 2009 956.9405'40922 C2009-901500-5

Second edition 2011

This book is dedicated to our mothers.
Both are pillars of strength, born near the Mediterranean Sea.
They are radiant in times of joy, resilient and supportive
in times of adversity . . . two friends who have never met.

Table of Contents

Acknowledgements

Many people believed in the importance of this book and the need for the voice of compassion to be heard, especially in light of recent developments in the Holy Land, Gaza in particular. Without their support, this book would not have been possible.

The authors are particularly indebted to David Ellis, who wrote most of Raouf Omar's stories as they were told to him. With patience and dedication, David edited all of our stories and coordinated a comprehensive review and editing effort. David also authored the story, "A Volunteer's Experience."

The stories "A Bus Ride in Galilee," "The Flower and the Tanker," "A Samsonite Bag Full of Dreams," and "The Lady from Bat Yam" were written as told to Mayssam Zaaroura. Mayssam captured exquisitely the message of the authors.

Special thanks to Monique Perrin d'Arloz, Anna Maranta, Yehudit Bernstein, Nicholas Trofimenkoff, Jane Bergin, Linda Dial, and Vanessa Wosik, whose belief in the book's importance, critical editorial input, and positive feedback added much value to the final manuscript.

Thanks to Robin Kinch, Karen Holmes, and Elizabeth Forbes for reviewing all the stories and whose continued support, constructive comments, and unwavering loyalty made David's job far more relevant and significantly enhanced the contents, while also reaffirming and validating the authors' voices.

The wonderful illustrations are the work of Raouf Omar, a man of many talents, executed with stained glass paint on Plexiglas.

Many thanks to our publisher, Tim Gordon, for his belief and support in this endeavour, and to Jane Karchmar, senior editor at GSPH, for giving us the confidence to complete this book.

Last but not least, our hearts go out to our families for their love, support, and encouragement.

RAOUF OMAR has no photographs from his life before emigrating to Canada; they were destroyed while he was in transit from Lebanon to Syria on his way to Canada during the 1982 war in Lebanon. The photos above show Palestinian refugees fleeing their homeland in 1948, and an early Palestinian refugee camp (*Wikipedia Commons*).

CLAUDE WEIL appears above in 1977 as a tanker in the Israeli army (left), and in boot camp in 1975 (right).

Biographical Notes

Raouf Omar is a Palestinian, born in March 1952 on the West Bank of the Jordan River, which, at that time, was part of Jordan. Since the Six Day War between Israel, Syria, Jordan, and Egypt, the West Bank was annexed by Israel. His family originates from Jaffa, a beautiful coastal city adjacent to Tel Aviv. In 1947, when the United Nations voted to partition the Holy Land into two countries, Israel and Palestine, war erupted. His family was driven out of its home. It settled in the Balata Camp managed and supplied by the United Nations.

Claude Weil is Jewish. He was born in April 1954 in Algeria, which was then a part of France since its colonization. His family originates from one of the twelve tribes of Israel that were scattered throughout the world following momentous historical events. In 1956, his family settled in France, as a colonial conflict was fast developing in Algeria. At the age of nineteen, having fully realized the scope and horror of what had happened to his people from antiquity through World War II and after, in a world still plagued with anti-Semitism, he decided to go back to Israel, which was fighting for acceptance by the Arab world. Most of the Palestinian people were caught in between in often very difficult conditions.

Raouf and Claude have been active participants in, and witnesses of, a tragedy that they believe can be resolved only by compassion grounded in fundamental human values, together with a good dose of realism, by all countries involved in the region. Today both Claude and Raouf live in Ottawa, Canada. Both families left behind a world they profoundly love, a tragically divided homeland – their homeland.

When Claude met Raouf in his restaurant, they embraced immediately as long-lost brothers. In each other's presence, their souls find some peace. They decided to write this book to celebrate the triumph of Compassion.

Foreword

How many times has one heard the valid statement: "One person can make a difference"? I believe these short stories by Claude Weil and Raouf Omar can perform a similar role in motivating people to become part of the solution rather than being a part of the problem. Raouf and Claude were participants in all the events depicted in these often harsh and emotional stories.

Historically, as Semitic people, Claude and Raouf share a common bond. Claude's maternal side of the family, the Dharmons, is a branch of the Haouara, Jewish Berbers who lived in Tunisia, Algeria, and Morocco. When Claude first entered Raouf's restaurant and saw Raouf's paintings of Jerusalem on the wall, he immediately "felt at home." Raouf is a Palestinian now living in Canada, while Claude is an Israeli also living in Canada. Both had very intense experiences in the Holy Land. Today they are the best of friends whose collaboration clearly demonstrates that people, no matter how diverse their individual backgrounds and experiences may be, can share similar values and ideals.

Their stories reflect a unifying theme, that of compassion. In a world increasingly subject to incompatible ideologies, warfare, global pandemics, and human suffering, the gift of human compassion is more essential than ever. Nurturing one's spirit is equally as important as health, food, and security. To be the recipient of an act of compassion forever changes one's soul and enhances the fellowship of humanity.

Claude's and Raouf's examples of human fortitude are tenderly portrayed. They convey the resiliency and poignancy of the human spirit. Amid adverse, hostile conditions there existed hope and joy—from a simple pleasure, or acts of compassion and generosity such as a fleeting glance, the gift of a Samsonite bag, or the warning of an impending sandstorm.

Both authors agreed to use the term Holy Land wherever possible and have tried to avoid political judgments, but do recognize historical fact as being an integral part of these stories. I believe their voices need to be heard and deserve a global audience.

It has been both a privilege and an honour to have been part of their endeavour.

For the reader who wants to know more about the Arab–Israeli conflict, references to a book and a Web site and its introductory lines can be found in the Appendix.

David O. Ellis

Raouf Omar, Claude Weil

Introduction

This is a tale of two people learning to see through their biases and joining forces to attempt to reach everyone who wants to see an end to the tragic conflict plaguing the Holy Land. One is an Israeli Jew, and the other, a Palestinian – two men who have developed a trusted friendship in Canada and who have become soul brothers, both living now far away from the suffering inflicted on so many.

Our moments together are a celebration of something stronger than friendship, as it is associated with an understanding of each other's trauma; compassion; and a dynamic creative force nourished by our Semitic background. We hope that as others read about our respective experiences, they will share our feelings.

We know that violence breeds violence; hatred breeds hatred. We also realize that this long history of violence and conflict will never solve the catastrophic problems facing the Holy Land. As it now stands, today's children of the Holy Land, and those of future generations, face a gloomy future of despair and destruction. We cannot afford to let the cycle of conflict and death continue. To do so would be to deny these children the chance to grow up following their dreams and aspirations. Their voices have to be heard rather than be usurped by those adults who have locked their horns in endless combat. We want all children to have the right to have smiles on their faces, to play without fear, to sail on the ocean, and to fly their kites in a pure, blue sky. We are not dreamers, not even peace activists; we are not here to suggest specific solutions. We just have our stories to tell, hoping that they may help.

We both have observed, through our respective experiences, that when unburdened, even for a moment, of the pressures of extremist ideologies and biases, Israelis and Palestinians have a natural affinity for goodness and peaceful, creative, harmonious living. We have been witnesses and even actors in many magical moments where this benevolence shone brightly. This is, in fact, true for most conflicts. Indeed, we could have focused on acts of brutalities we have also witnessed, but what good would it do?

Our respective experiences have been summarized into short stories of goodwill between Israeli Arabs, Israeli Jews, Palestinians, Bedouins, and even British nuns. Each story represents a dim, fragile light of hope in the long, dark tunnel of violence. To Israeli and Palestinian leaders, we are simply saying: "Please take note of these dim lights, for many of your people have stories similar to ours and often have suffered more than we did . . . Sit together, you who also have suffered, and keep on drawing the contours of two viable states, which, together, will be an example for the rest of the world – a rainbow of peace, a spectrum of colours, illuminating the land, bringing life, joy, and lasting peace."

To other countries in the Middle East and the Western World, we say: "Let go of your personal political agendas. We are such a small part of the world, and we have suffered too much, like roosters forced to fight; be truly generous and help us in our quest. You may very well be the main beneficiaries of a long and lasting peace in the Holy Land, as even darker destructive forces may be looming on the horizon."

Let us all be allies in peace . . . *shalom* . . . *salaam*. Do we really have a choice? If we fail, the rest of the planet may also fail . . . we are the people of the Holy Land, its guardians, a place where the one and only G-d[1] decided that this was where humanity would begin.

---

1 Most faiths have some written way of showing respect for the Sacred. Observant Jews normally avoid writing any name of G-d casually because of the risk that it may later be defaced, obliterated, or destroyed accidentally, which is prohibited within our belief system.

A Family's Journey

Raouf Omar

A Family's Journey

I was born in the refugee camp of Balata, located just north of Nablus on the West Bank of the Jordan. This is now occupied territory as a result of The Six Day War of June 1967. The camp was established in 1950 under the United Nations' protection. This was my home: concrete structures, the same dimensions as the tents they had replaced, formed alleyways so narrow that large people cannot walk along them. It reminds me of those oppressive structures scientists build for rats to scurry, to and fro, in the pursuit of some academic discovery. Today, a bird flying overhead would see one of the most densely populated areas on Earth with over thirty thousand people living in less than two square kilometres. This was the only world I knew. This was my life.

With the defeat of Turkey in World War One, the Ottoman Empire was partitioned. France occupied Syria and Lebanon. Britain took Palestine, Transjordan, and Iraq. Under the British mandate, thousands of Jews moved to Palestine, encouraged by The Balfour Declaration of 1917, which established the idea of a future homeland. By 1947, most Arab states had achieved independence; Transjordan became Jordan, but Palestine had remained under British control. Arab resentment and hostility towards the British for allowing the Jewish influx into Palestine often turned violent; for example, the vicious general strike of 1936. This was my parents' world. This was the climate that precipitated the event forcing my family to flee.

It was a hot summer day in Balata, the streets crowded with kids, as the streets were the children's only playground. I was around eleven or twelve years old, I cannot remember exactly, sitting at the table next to my mother with my hand under my chin. She was a professional seamstress and was repairing my worn shirt so that I could go back outside to play. I have always been curious by nature. I suddenly looked at her with passionate, yet sad, eyes and surprised her by asking a question – one that had been on my mind for a long time.

"Why do you limp when you walk?" I asked. I needed an answer, as no other woman around walked with a limp. My mother was a beautiful woman, both in mind and body. Her skin was light chocolate in colour but not dark; she had thick, long, black hair and eyes that could melt your heart. She looked at me.

"Why do you want to know?" she asked.

"I want to see you the same as the other women, walking normal," I replied. She stopped working, fixing those magnificent eyes upon me.

"Don't you want to go outside?" she said, attempting to distract me.

"No," I quickly answered. Mother gazed off into the distance, then grabbed my hand and began to speak in a voice full of emotion.

"It was 1947, and we were living in the beautiful coastal Palestinian city of Jaffa. It is believed to be one of the world's oldest cities. The British soldiers stormed into our house and arrested your father and your uncle. This was the start of our journey.

A British soldier had been killed, and your father and uncle, along with a group of other Palestinians, were put in jail.

"Who killed the British soldier?" they wanted to know. Interrogation and torture were to no avail. Nobody knew. Dissatisfied, they now stated that one member of the group had committed the murder, and, shortly thereafter, every day, they randomly took two of the prisoners outside, stood them in front of the rest and shot them. They intended to force a confession. These were innocent men. Yes, they had previously protested, non-violently, against the British authorities over the loss of their freedom, and yes, they wanted to become an independent nation. Your father's and uncle's situation was grave. They were in fear for their lives; they didn't know if it would be their turn the next day.

While incarcerated, and both knowing how to maintain water pumps, they were put in charge of repairing the jail's unreliable water pumps. This afforded them an opportunity, early one morning, to escape into an adjoining field. Although discovered and shot at, they managed, under the cover of darkness, to make it back to their home.

Panic-stricken and desperate not to be caught, knowing full well that it was only a question of time before the British soldiers would be at the house to arrest all the members of their family, they begged your grandparents to run away with them and to leave the frequent bloodshed behind, caused both by the hands of the British Authority and by Jewish youth gangs. Your grandfather, who was blind, refused to go with them. Perhaps, he believed he might have been a liability, jeopardizing our slim chance of escape. I don't know. To him it probably made no difference."

To this day, his fate remains unknown. Later on, some people told us that he had fallen into a hole and died. This has never been confirmed.

My mother continued her story. "We fled, heading in the direction of Jordan, looking for a safe haven, and luckily we managed to find travel in a truck, a very unsafe truck speeding along as we were trying to escape. Was fate conspiring against us? It crashed and rolled over, severely fracturing my femur."

As a child I could only try to imagine how my parents must have felt; hope turning to despair, then panic, the terror of being caught, my mother's physical condition, and the extreme pain she must have been feeling. What were they going to do? I sat there mesmerized, stunned.

"Fortune must have been smiling upon us," my mother continued. "We were able to get to a missionary hospital located nearby. A hospital run by British nuns, no less! The irony of it all, we would have nothing to fear, because the nuns would not turn us over to the British authorities. Although the hospital was in a primitive condition and was limited in its resources, the nuns provided me with the best care they could offer. We would never forget their assistance! Rest and security were more precious than gold! They made me comfortable and did what they could, but gangrene set in. The head nun told your father they either had to amputate my leg or I would die. My husband didn't know what to do, overwhelmed by the situation, my extreme pain, and the rapid deterioration in my health. Our situation was grim. Our future uncertain, unknown, as we had no money, nowhere to go, no hope. His difficult, heart-wrenching decision was to let me die.

"Now, your father was not a particularly religious man, but he decided to pray for me. His prayers must have been heard! We were informed by the nuns that an Arab herbalist lived nearby and that he could possibly help. Our good fortune continued! He came daily and he skillfully applied his knowledge until miraculously I was healed. I could walk again. We were then able to continue our quest for safety, culminating with our arrival in Balata, a United Nations-protected refugee camp. We had tents over our heads—we were safe at last! Another life had begun." At that moment my eyes were full of tears. I hugged her, thanked her for the shirt, and ran out to play.

Life was not easy for my parents or for any of the thousands of other families there. Life in tents, rationed food, second-hand clothes, and loss of dignity were the norm. For many, sex was the only "gift," the only goodness in their lives. The resulting children meant a larger, stronger family, and a few years later, I was born in one of those tents. Later, they moved into one of the cell-like concrete block houses. My mother managed to earn some money as a seamstress, but it was never enough.

The Palestinian plight seemed erased from the Western mind, but not from that of the Palestinian. Anger became a genetic trait. We focused our anger into getting on with our lives rather than fighting against Israel. Education became the key to the future! Education could replace everything we had lost! This is why Palestinians hold more degrees than any people from any other Middle Eastern country. Sweet sweat; it's what dreams are made of!

But without the compassion shown by those British nuns in that missionary hospital, so many years ago, there would be no stories for me to tell.

Claude Weil

Letter to Raouf

My Dear Friend,

You and I come from two opposite camps that have fought bitterly for over seventy years in the Holy Land. Then, why is it that the moment you, the Palestinian, and I, the Israeli, met in your restaurant, we immediately bonded and hugged like two best friends who have been separated by life for years?

I knew you were one of ours. As I discovered your art, lining the walls of your corner of Holy Land, I was back home.

By "one of ours," I mean a member of my maternal family, the Dharmons. The Dharmons have lived in Algeria, Tunisia, and Morocco since they left Israel following the destruction of the first temple and of the second temple by Titus the Roman. We have known exile through Italy and Spain. We are known as a branch of the Haouara Berber tribe, where we were called Dharmon. The famous Arab writer Ibn-Khaldun documented the existence and life of the Jewish Berbers.

We have in common life in the Arab world, around the Mediterranean, centuries of life under the sun, in arid lands with tribal rituals regulating our lives. We have a hefty respect for what nature provides for us to live simple lives under one G-d. The quest for water and for trading routes has often shaped the path of our journeys and the location of our villages. We have a sense of the harmonies of colours, the poetry of words, and the music that reflect the vast, unforgiving deserts, the red mountain ranges, and the deep blue uniting sea and sky. Our men are proud and family oriented; our women are gorgeous and creative, and display an unshakable optimism during the most adverse times. No one uses spices like they do—in every aspect of life! Their rich smiles are like the sun, and their dark eyes forever mysterious.

We also have differences—such as elements of our faith—but most of the time we lived for centuries together in happy symbiosis.

In fact, sometimes we flourished together, such as in the golden era of the Islamic Empire in Spain, where our complementary qualities were at the roots of great developments in the arts, humanities, agriculture, and scientific discoveries. During the time of the Ottoman Empire, Jews and Palestinians lived in harmony side by side in the Holy Land. Sometimes we were loving brothers, and sometimes we were unloving brothers; nevertheless, as Semitic people, we were brothers.

I can illustrate this with the role of my maternal grandfather in World War One. My grandfather and his five brothers, born in French Algeria, fought for France against the Germans on all fronts. Three died as a consequence of gas attacks and complicated injuries.

My grandfather wore very thick glasses and could not be a combat soldier. Instead, he was in charge of the welfare of many colonial troops: Pieds Noirs, as the French Algerians were called, and many Muslim soldiers from Algeria, Morocco, and Tunisia, who all fought like lions. Men from the vast plains, mountain ranges, and deserts of North Africa had been, in a matter of weeks, propelled from their homes to a hell of cold, mud, and death in northern and eastern France.

My grandfather, who spoke perfect Arabic, assisted Muslim troops in every way possible. He made sure these men were not served pork, could pray, and wrote letters home for them. He consoled them. He arranged places for them to visit during leaves, as otherwise there was no place for them to go. Many would never again see their white, sunny villages.

His kindness to these Muslim troops was returned during World War Two. Vichy France actively collaborated with the Germans occupying France. Anti-Semitic rules were extended to Algeria, a French colony. As Jews, my maternal grandmother and grandfather were fired from their government jobs. My mother, then thirteen years old, was expelled from her school. Only a year before, she had sung for the president of France, as she was a talented, budding opera singer. She came to school one morning. A list of all the Jewish kids had been posted . . . To make matters worse, the German Africa Corps, led by Rommel, was getting closer to Algeria.

Thankfully, my grandfather was given an accountant job by an Arab merchant, a friend of his. He was able to feed his family. Furthermore, an Arab farmer was ready to hide his family if the Germans entered Algeria. Things were far worse for my father, who lived in France.

Letter to Raouf

Do you see the irony of it all, my dear friend?

Later, in 1956, as the conflict heated up in Algeria between France and the native population, both my grandparents, being French civil servants, moved us to France, as they saw the end of France in Algeria coming quickly. Both the British and French Empire had started crumbling after World War Two. As my grandfather and his family climbed onto the ship that would take them to France, they left behind the memory of just and decent people, Arabs and non-Arabs alike. In 1961, my twenty-nine-year-old uncle, who had a PhD in philosophy from the Sorbonne University, was called back from France to fight in Algeria. He was French, but had immense difficulties fighting against the Arab kids he had grown up with, playing soccer in the streets of Constantine. He eventually perished in a French hospital at the end of his two-year tour. My mother still has the letters in which he described the horror of this war that had become so personal for him.

By the time I was eighteen, in 1972, I seriously questioned why we were living in France at all, after what had happened to my family in World War Two and later. By then, most Jews from the Arab world had gone back to Israel, which their ancestors had left centuries before. For many surviving Jews after World War Two and for Jews expelled from Arab countries after the partition of Palestine and the Six Day War, Israel was their only hope, although some chose to go to countries such as France.

When I arrived there in 1973, during the Yom Kippur War, I felt I had finally arrived home. Everything around me spoke of home, the people, the customs, the scents, and the people, Jews or Arabs.

Here is the real meaning of this tragedy; I really was back home – back to the land of my ancestors from which they had been forced out many years ago – but you had lost yours. Again, it is not the purpose of this book to argue about right and wrong. In fact, as you know, my dear brother, you and I have set our sights well above that. We also know that this conflict will finally stop if Jews and Palestinians agree to remind the world that they are so close as people that they must decide on their own terms that the plow has to replace the sword. Our destinies, in this land blessed by G-d, are intertwined for eternity. There is no choice.

I would like you to know that I, with a friend, personally buried, with great respect and sadness, the skeletal remains of a warrior from a past time – we think an Egyptian soldier from the Six Day War – during a night patrol near a hellish base called Bi'r Hasanah. We did not know the proper protocol. We did our best. I often wonder who the mother of this soldier was. So many mothers hurt in the Holy Land.

I will finish with the following anecdote.

It normally took me as long as seven hours and many cars to hitchhike my way home to the kibbutz from my Sinai posting. As you know, Israeli soldiers were not picked up by Arab Israelis. That can be understood.

Well, one night, I was stuck near Haifa because of some kind of security alert. I was very late in reaching the Meron crossroad. It was past three a.m. I had to be back in my unit by noon the next day. I started running the last fifteen kilometres or so to my kibbutz, but knew I would not make it . . . I had run out of luck.

At that very moment, a Peugeot utility vehicle passed me at full speed, and I knew it was going to a nearby Arab village. Then I saw the brake light come on. I ran like a madman. The Arab driver lowered his window and asked me if I was from Kibbutz Sasa. I said, "Yes." He took me on board. He had had a friend for many years in Sasa; in fact, since the early days of the kibbutz. He drove past the turn to his village and dropped me at the security gate of my kibbutz.

One hour later, I was on my way back. I had hugged Betty and spent twenty minutes watching our son, Raphael, sleep.

This book's fundamental message is that you and I, through our personal experiences, are the proof that we can live in peace together. Oh yes, my dear friend, there will be peace . . . someday.

Claude

Claude Weil

How Sweet

As I started feeling nauseous, I wondered if I would make it to Kibbutz Regavim.

It was 1974. Since November 1973, I had been living at Kibbutz Ein Hashofet. My roommate was Claude. Throughout the winter, we had developed a friendship that is still vibrant to this day. We spent the rainy winter season getting to know each other. By April, Claude and his girlfriend had moved to Kibbutz Regavim, fifteen kilometres or so from Ein Hashofet. On Shabbat, I occasionally paid them a visit; we traded books, talked about spirituality, war, peace, and had many good laughs. To reach them, I hitchhiked about six kilometres and then walked another eight kilometres across farmland. Vineyards would welcome me the closer I came to the kibbutz.

This was the first time I had walked the eight kilometres in summer, and I was not doing well. The noon sun was like a hammer on my head. The temperature was around forty degrees Celsius.

My side bag was heavy with wet books, as they had crushed my plastic water bottle. I had assumed that I could easily walk the remaining six kilometres or so without this water. I had no hat. All the elements were in place for trouble.

What I later learnt in boot camp was that once dehydration grabs you under such hot and dry conditions, death could follow fairly rapidly unless water was quickly found and consumed. One of our sergeants never ceased to remind us about the importance of drinking frequently during our long walks. He had learnt his lesson the hard way. He had lost his brother to dehydration a couple of years earlier. They had run out of water, and suddenly his brother had collapsed. He sat his brother under a tree and ran to look for help, which he found quickly. When he and a group of men returned with the precious water to help his brother, it was too late. Dehydration can be fairly advanced before external signs, such as dizziness and headaches, manifest themselves. It varies from one person to another.

I continued walking towards the kibbutz, knowing my situation was serious. I was developing a headache, my tongue was dry and heavy, my vision blurred. The landscape was beginning to undulate in front of me. I was moving on automatic pilot. I tried to remember how much I had drunk before leaving Ein Hashofet. I came up with nothing . . . My mind started to meander between then and now. Why did I start thinking of work and the Hebrew classes with Sarah, a wonderful teacher? We sat along tables forming a large rectangle. I was continuously called upon for assistance by two friends from France, Alain and Gérard, as they hardly studied after classes. They were too busy dating volunteers from around the world. In addition, as neither of them spoke English, I had to translate for them and their Juliet of the day. One day, getting tired of it all, I wrote above Alain's bed what to say to a girl in English to ensure success – as if I knew! That evening he looked for me for a long time, having told his latest conquest, a pretty Californian: "You look ugly and fat." Gérard and I were hiding behind bushes when Alain rushed out of his room screaming for revenge.

The trail was going uphill now. The effort far more demanding. How much did I drink before leaving the kibbutz? I tried hard to recollect . . . there was a coffee at breakfast before I went to work. No, I did not go to work. It was the Sabbath. My forehead was burning. I wrapped my shirt around it. Again, while walking, I lost track of the present as my mind drifted.

I was now focusing on my painting job in the electric factory. I painted transformers for four hours, and then Kato, a volunteer from Japan, would take over for four hours, allowing me to attend classes with other immigrants. At the end of each shift, we reported on a board, attached to a pillar, how many transformers we had painted. No matter how hard I worked, he always painted more than I did. Near the spray-painting hood, there was a work station for older kibbutz members where they could work sitting down. They treated me like a son. I was sitting with them at coffee breaks. They were all heroes of the war of independence, but remained humble.

They used my Hebrew name: "Chaim, you work very hard and you already paint far more transformers than anyone we have seen at this workstation, but listen, no one here can focus like Kato."

How Sweet

A few months later, as Kato and I became friends, I understood better the inner calm and focus that rituals such as meditation brought to my friend. In the evening, he could spend hours in the lotus position. Sometimes he played the flute in this position. It was magical. This pure sound rising into the night was deeply moving. I learnt from him some elements of Eastern wisdom and practices, but would never reach his level of serenity and focus.

I came back to my senses for a few seconds. My legs were heavy, too heavy. I was barely able to move. Oh yes, how much had I drunk before leaving the kibbutz? No matter how hard I tried, I could not maintain my train of thought.

Suddenly, I heard a rumbling and voices. Two men grabbed me by the shoulders, held me, and had me sit against the wheel of a wagon. They spoke in Arabic. Then I felt water on my lips, at first just a trickle. I also felt cold water on my chest, my cheeks, my neck, and my forehead. Never had any liquid tasted so exquisite! I asked for more water. They told me in Hebrew to wait a moment, that it could hurt me to drink too much too fast. Sip after sip, they gave me more water. I was gaining strength and managed to stand up.

Their wagon was loaded with watermelons. They split one and we shared it.

They were older, their faces radiating kindness and generosity. I understood they were field workers, simple men who worked very hard. My face was all sticky with the sugar of the watermelon.

"You are a strong man. You are fine now," one said in broken Hebrew. My own Hebrew was not much better. "It is forbidden to travel without water. You need a lot of water always when you walk in the sun . . . You are going to Regavim." This was not a question. The trail was leading to Regavim. They, sitting on top of a wagon pulled by two mules, had come upon me at a fortuitous moment. I sat with them, relieved, but feeling rather stupid about my lack of preparation for dealing with the heat. They had saved me from an extremely serious life-threatening situation.

"You had almost arrived. Look, the vineyards are just ahead of us. Two more kilometres and we will be selling our watermelons, starting with Regavim."

The two men were dressed in black pants and shirts with green caps, military style. Their skin was cracked from years in the sun, toiling in the fields. How much history had they seen while working in their watermelon patches and delivering to whoever would buy the fruits of their labour: Turks, British, Israelis, and obviously their fellow Palestinians. I looked around. The vineyards were gorgeous; each individual green grape was like a small egg. At my request, they stopped, and I picked two large bunches. One we shared, the other was for Claude. A token of gratitude for what they had given me – perhaps my life.

Sixteen months later, I was on a desert evening patrol in the Negev. The rocky land was still warm. Not a single noise came from my water bottle. The rule was to share a full water bottle with our tent mate so that one bottle would be completely full as the other one was empty.

As we walked stealthily in one column under a full moon, I remembered . . . I remembered the grapes.

They were full of a sweet, thick juice. They melted in the mouth. G-d, how sweet that land could be.

Claude Weil

A Bus Ride in Galilee

How could I forget the fall of 1975?

Long after the hot and humid nights of summer had faded into the blustery winds of fall, as winter crept ever closer, I found myself with seven other Israelis from my kibbutz as part of a Garin – a group of youths aspiring to become Kibbutz members.

Our home, Kibbutz Sasa, was located five kilometres south of the Lebanese border near one of Israel's highest peaks: Mount Meron, in Galilee. Were you to stand on that peak, the Lebanese border would stretch in the distance and the depth of the Galilee region with its unique flora and fauna, found nowhere else in Israel, would lie at your feet.

However, at that moment, we were far from home. We were thick in the middle of boot camp, somewhere in Central Israel. Our days and nights were a blur of excruciatingly difficult training, seven-minute meals, and four-hour nights in cold tents, interrupted by one hour of guard duty. And there was the November rain . . . cold and relentless.

The drill sergeants were making sure that we were resilient combat soldiers, stretching our physical endurance to levels we did not even know we could reach. They yelled orders at the top of their lungs, pushing us into unknown regions of what the body and the mind could sustain. They tested our nerves to ensure that if we were to break, it would not happen in the midst of combat but here in this camp, surrounded by eucalyptus trees.

It was a time with no cellular phones or e-mail to connect us to the outside world. Daily conditions that were Spartan to the extreme were all part of our training.

We were young, but our intense camaraderie was the last reminder of the world we had left in our kibbutz. We had to learn to kill. There was no choice. We had a small country and our families to defend.

A Bus Ride in Galilee

Yet we hoped we would never have to use our military skills. Veterans from all armies know the burden they have to carry long after they have performed their duty. Mothers on all sides had bleeding hearts, hoping that perhaps the loss of a son or a husband had not been in vain.

Still at war with many of its Arab neighbours following the clash of forces in the Yom Kippur war, Israel was engulfed in sadness following the loss of so many of its youth. Its government was determined to build an even mightier army to sign honorable peace treaties recognizing its existence, or, if necessary . . . to win the next war. Fragile ceasefires were keeping the armies apart.

We were dedicated kibbutzniks being turned into dedicated soldiers. We were required to be in a state of constant readiness, as peace treaties had yet to find their way to the table with any of the surrounding nations.

The sergeants shared our misery. We admired them. "Difficult in training, easier in war"—this was the motto under which we were trained to defend Israel.

"Home-leaves" were virtually non-existent, but as if the fates understood our need, we were given one day. We donned our A uniforms, ready to leave. A palpable tension permeated the camp as each soldier awaited a last-minute development that could deprive us from seeing those we loved in the next twenty-four hours. My fiancée, Betty, was finishing her last year of study in Toronto, Canada, but I was looking forward with anticipation to spending time with our adoptive parents in the kibbutz; Gilan had graduated as an electrical engineer at the age of fifty-two after setting up the kibbutz in 1949. Shulamit was the post office master.

I could not wait for a cup of hot tea and some sweets. I could almost taste them. I just wanted to be sitting in their small living room, in a one-bedroom apartment. They had never been blessed with children but had treated Betty and me like their own.

Gilan was a lanky fellow, with a brilliant mind that worked endlessly under a serene surface. Shulamit was a round and jovial ball of energy, a perfect balance to her husband. I could hardly wait.

The buses that were commissioned by the military arrived to pick us up from the base. When we were finally ensconced in the small seats, relief flooded through me . . . we were a little closer to arriving home.

Our bus snaked its way to Haifa, and there we transferred onto an "Egged"[2] bus that was usually stationed at our kibbutz at night and driven by a kibbutz member who had been a sailor on the *Exodus 1947*—a ship that left the shores of France in the year it was named after, carrying the first load of Jewish emigrants, mostly Holocaust survivors, to Palestine.

The driver had proudly shown us his Palestinian passport, issued under the British mandate, but there were no fond memories about his internment in Cyprus. Now his job was to drive that route daily and, at the end of each day, he would park the Egged bus near the communal dining room at the kibbutz. There he would enjoy his meal with his family and later lay his head to sleep in his tiny apartment, perhaps dreaming of extraordinary days past as one of the founders of the kibbutz in 1949.

We transferred buses and immediately proceeded to do what every soldier in training does in such a situation—we fell asleep. It would take about two hours for the final leg home, driving up through Akko and through the wonderful hills of Galilee to our kibbutz.

What seemed like a short time later, but in fact had been the better part of an hour, I was jerked awake by a commotion. The bus had ground to a halt in Akko, a wonderful port town nestled across from Haifa Bay. Betty and I used to stroll here in the evening and eat fish by the sea in a restaurant owned by an Arab-Israeli man. He had a large moustache and a wonderful outlook on life. I delighted in the dark olives, hot peppers, hummus, fresh pita bread, and the fresh fish caught that same day. All this seemed like a long time ago, yet it had been only three months since my last visit.

Now, I was wearing my green uniform, an M16 automatic rifle in hand, one of many contained in a huge, oily bag unloaded from a truck. They should have been sent to Vietnam, but were probably sent to us during the Yom Kippur war.

Returning to the present, I sat in a daze staring at a group of young Palestinian women as they boarded the bus. To this day, I cannot say if they were Muslims or Christians. They were all wearing the same shiny green jackets. Ironically, I thought, there was little difference between civilian and soldier. Our winter coats were somewhat larger, longer, and thicker, as we had to endure some seriously cold nights.

---

2 The Israeli national bus company.

The bus pulled away from Akko, continuing on its journey as the drizzling rain covered the countryside in a curtain of mist and grey. My fellow soldier, Moshe, sat alone. He had slept through the delay, his head leaning on the bus's rattling window. One of the Palestinian women sat down in the empty seat beside him, while the others were scattered throughout the heaving vehicle, skillfully driven by the aging sailor of the *Exodus*.

I'm not sure why I was intrigued by the sight of my friend Moshe and this young Palestinian girl on those little seats. All I could see of them was the contrast of tousled blond hair, a fall of a thick black mane, and occasionally very thin elegant fingers. Moshe's sleep was fitful. In his stupor, he was trying to find a comfortable position – a place where his sleep would be more peaceful. One moment, his head would loll to rest on the rounded curve of the girl's green-clad shoulder. The next it would roll back toward the window and the vibrating rhythm of the bus. I, mesmerized, watched this happen a few times. My gaze kept dancing between my friend's head and the rigid, straight back of the girl. I could not see her face but she sat immobile as Moshe tilted back and forth like a lilting ship.

I could see the nozzle of Moshe's M16 sticking through his knees, both his hands holding it in a grip that was tight even in sleep. The bus started climbing through the verdant hills, slowly winding its way higher on the snaky road. Most of the landscape's details were blurred behind the wall of drizzle and before my own exhausted eyes. I remained fascinated by the tableau unfolding before me, by Moshe's search for comfort, and the cloak of dignity surrounding the young woman. Suddenly, Moshe's head settled heavily – once and for all – on the girl's shoulder, his blond spikes of hair almost touching the smooth olive of her cheek. Slowly, I could see Moshe's agitation seeping out of his body and his left side sinking into the girl's warmth. She did not move.

A while later, as the bus rumbled over the rough streets of a small town, Moshe began to stir, tensing with the vibration of the heavy beast beneath us. This is when, incredulously, I watched the girl carefully extract her arm from between their bodies and stretch it over my Israeli friend's shoulder, curving it around him and cradling him tenderly.

By then, my senses were screamingly awake. I could feel the adrenalin wash through my veins, waking my nerve endings and raising the hair on my arms. I sat up and looked at our fellow passengers. At least two of the girl's friends were aware of what was happening. They observed calmly, barely exchanging a word or two – none of which I could understand.

Time passed, and my senses must have been lulled back to sleep, because once again I was jarred awake. We had neared the Meron crossroad that would lead us to Kibbutz Sasa. The bus heaved to the left before speeding up for the last twenty minutes of the journey.

My eyes were inexorably drawn to Moshe and the young woman. They remained locked together in this quasi-embrace. Moshe must have spent at least one hour held in the gentle cradle of the woman's arm, before all too soon the bus came to a halt near an Arab-Israeli village. I noticed some of the young Palestinian women rising to disembark.

Moshe stirred awake, lifting himself upright. The young girl barely moved, despite arriving at her destination. The Israeli soldier looked the young Palestinian squarely in the face; she shyly tilted her body round toward him, all the while avoiding his sharp gaze. She gently removed her arm from behind him. Her friends stood outside in the little drizzle, huddled together the way women do, pulling their hoods over their hair. They waited patiently. I watched with my face plastered against the cold window.

As she walked down the aisle and stepped into the rain, the girl did not pull up her hood. This is when I first saw her face; I saw her wonderfully defined features, large black eyes beneath jet-black winged eyebrows. She stood, letting the gleaming drops of rain roll down the jet waterfall of hair, her face tilted toward the window where Moshe sat. His eyes remained trained on hers. None of her friends said a word, and I held my breath. To this day, I don't know what Moshe and that girl shared in that one gaze. But I knew something extraordinary had happened between an Israeli boy and a Palestinian girl.

Twenty minutes later, I was still recovering as the bus crossed the security gates of the Kibbutz. I made my way to my little apartment, which felt so empty without Betty, who was studying in Canada. I quickly dropped my small bag and rifle before heading back out. Tomorrow I would have to worry about repacking my five pairs of socks and five pairs of underwear – my only real belongings – into five plastic bags so that the desert sand would not worm its way into the nooks and crannies and add its grainy grit. I would have to remember a box of talcum powder, having experienced thirty-kilometres runs, carrying a man on a stretcher and sand rubbing along my joints. I knew better now. I was a seasoned soldier at this point. I walked quickly to Gilan and Shulamit's home, through the meandering lanes of our kibbutz. I knocked on the yellow door and a blast of warmth hit me as it swung open. Gilan's gentle eyes welcomed me home, as Shulamit's voice rejoiced in my safe return. It was only later, at night, in the solitude of my small apartment, that I let my mind return to the Egged bus and that ride across Galilee.

My M16 was safely locked in my cabinet, the fully loaded magazines in a separate place, my still-wet uniform hung in the bathroom; the oil stove warmed the cold tiles.

I stared at the ceiling for a while, thinking of the two souls who for one brief moment shared a modicum of peace without speaking a word. I thought of Betty and her warm smile and surrendered finally to the seeking fingers of sleep.

Raouf Omar

A Samsonite Bag Full of Dreams

I was in my early twenties, a youth full of hopes and dreams for my future. I was saving money to pay for university.

As a Palestinian, working within Israel's Green Line was the only chance of making a decent living. I was able to hoard away some of my hard-earned money for school; the rest I gave to my family. Every day I would make the journey from Balata, my home, a refugee camp in the West Bank, and travel for hours to Israel with the thousands of others like me, stopping at the checkpoints of the day. Those checkpoints were the symbol of the most depressing thing in our lives: we were refugees in our own country.

Balata is the largest camp in the West Bank, crowded with over 20,000 refugees. It was a community active in Palestinian politics, both *intifadas*[3] and human rights.

But like many of the hordes of refugees in the West Bank, I was earning my living in Ramat Gan, a city close to Tel Aviv, working in a mattress factory making the sponge filling. It certainly wasn't glamorous or exciting, but it was a job, and as a Palestinian with few prospects, I couldn't complain. I worked there for six months whenever I could find the time, saving whatever I made for school.

The factory owner was a man named Shaoul. He and his brother, Manahem, were partners and as different as day and night.

Manahem was a schoolteacher and was the younger of the two, but you wouldn't have figured that out watching the two together. They

3 *Intifada* is an Arabic word for *shaking off*, though it is generally translated into English as rebellion or *uprising*. The First Intifada, a Palestinian uprising against Israeli rule, occurred from 1987 to 1993. The Second, or al-Aqsa Intifada, is the violent Palestinian–Israeli conflict that began in September 2000. http://en.wikipedia.org/wiki/Intifada

A Samsonite Bag Full of Dreams

were both old, with identical shocks of white hair. I remember Shaoul as a very decent man, but with a wicked, short temper. Whenever someone would piss him off, he'd start jumping up and down in a tantrum; it would crack me up . . . but he was a straight shooter all the way. You always knew where you stood with him.

Manahem, in contrast, was a down-to-earth, quiet man, always calm; but the kind of calm where you knew something was brewing under the surface. He didn't speak much, but he would get angry at his brother for the smallest of mistakes. They never argued, but Shaoul could tell when Manahem was mad at something. A small smile would dance briefly on his face. That always baffled me.

The factory was an industrial hub, in an industrial age. Everyone wore gas masks because of the chemical fumes. You'd cook a bunch of chemicals together, and the sponge would rise like a loaf of fresh-baked bread.

The mask was too hot. I would sneak it off my face sometimes for a breath of fresh air – well, as fresh as I could find within that factory. It was a dangerous move, but I didn't care.

Shaoul and I had a good relationship – not easy for an Israeli and a Palestinian at the best of times. But he liked me; I was always on time and I worked hard. He knew I was saving for school. At the time, I had applied to the University of Cairo to study Fine Arts or Physical Training. I was a good student and I had high hopes for myself – I had ranked eleventh in the whole West Bank for grades.

But . . . I was told art was for losers, so I also applied to study Commerce. One day, I read my name in the morning paper! I'd been accepted to university – to study Commerce. That's where I was heading at the end of the summer. Although outwardly I may have appeared calm and emotionless, inwardly I felt proud. Not just for me, but also for my family, as everything we had achieved was from nothing. My university acceptance meant an economic boost for them. I would be able to provide support for my younger siblings' schooling.

All too soon, the time came to start the next stage in my life. The time came for me to say goodbye to Shaoul and his factory and to make my way to Cairo. I was already late for admissions, so I told Shaoul I would be leaving the following day. He nodded briefly and said, "Okay, no problem." Then he told me he was leaving for the afternoon and headed downtown with his brother.

But, one hour later, he was back. I looked up as he walked towards me. He told me to quit what I was doing and come to his office.

My heart started pounding. I could see other workers coming in from the surrounding factories and it scared the hell out of me. What was going on? Why was everyone here?

I walked slowly towards his office and opened the door. All I could see were faces, the smiling faces of friends and colleagues. They were all crammed into Shaoul's office, standing obediently around a table laden with a cake, juice, and burning candles.

I looked into Shaoul's eyes and he smiled. I remember his words clearly to this day. He told me he was sad that I was leaving. "You're a hard worker; I'll be sad to see you go. But I can't stop you from getting an education."

I stood there, dumbstruck. It was a small gesture, but no one had ever cared enough to acknowledge my hopes and dreams like that before. Amid cheers and laughter, we had ourselves a little party!

Suddenly, Shaoul stood up and he pulled out a box from under his desk. He slid it over to me across the table and I stared at it hard before tearing open the cardboard. It was a Samsonite case. I had never owned anything so expensive before. And it was loaded down with pens, papers, a calculator . . . and double the wages for that week.

My throat closed up and my vision blurred.

"Go! Start your education," he said.

To this day, a successful business owner, an artist, a father, and a happy man . . . I still have that bag.

Claude Weil

The Shepherd

I slowly opened my eyes. Every part of my body was hurting, but I was rested. Where was I? What was I doing in this trench at dawn?

My mind jolted back to the reality of my situation. I had fallen asleep in my dug trench in the middle of the night's training . . . I cautiously looked around. All I could see were empty trenches, those individual holes we had been ordered to dig in the middle of the night. My squad of twelve was gone. We had just spent twenty-four hours learning various camouflage techniques, transforming ourselves into trees or other landscape features in order to blend in. Then we had practised the art of stealth until, as a cold rain started, we ended up concealed in the land in the one-man trenches.

I collected my gear and extracted myself from the wet, muddy, and slippery manhole.

I was absolutely lost, somewhere on top of a mountain covered in small trees and shrubs. This was the second month of boot camp, a blur of strenuous training, emotional pressure, and three- to four-hour nights interrupted by guard duties.

I had coped well, as I was receiving a steady stream of precious letters from Betty.

But now, my world was upside down. My buddies had left me behind, despite all the precautions we took at night to conduct regular head counts while walking in a column of soldiers sufficiently spaced out to avoid falling as one in the event of an ambush. Obviously, it did not work out as well as planned when we dug ourselves into our individual holes.

The chain of mountains' beauty at sunrise, with more and more details emerging from the landscape, was the only heartwarming aspect of the situation. My uniform and helmet appeared to be smoking as the sun rapidly warmed up the air, changing the water in my sodden clothes to steam.

The rest of my emotion was pure fear: fear of not finding my way; fear of eventually having to face my captain and being severely punished for losing my position, probably by having to remain in camp during a rare leave, in a week's time. I would then have to wait for up to another six weeks for a similar opportunity.

"What are you doing all alone, soldier?" I jumped, even though the question had been uttered in a gentle but firm voice. I turned around. Facing me was an Arab shepherd, his black and white goats well back, grazing among the shrubs.

He wore a long, white, full-length robe and a black vest. His facial features, under his small white turban, were very sharp, with well-defined cheekbones, a thin nose, and shiny black eyes.

He held a knotty wooden cane. I held an M16 automatic rifle and still wore my helmet, which I removed and hung on my infantry belt, which held magazines.

What a contrast! I had managed to compose myself and looked like a soldier in control. I was not. Perhaps he knew.

Now, we had an interesting situation, as we were in a military zone strictly off limits to civilians. He obviously did not feel that way; he probably had been roaming that mountain range for many years with his goats and saw no reason to change.

We both had a problem. He had been found and had reason for concern. I was lost and had as many reasons to be concerned.

My duty was to report him immediately. I locked eyes with him and then gave up. I just could not picture myself escorting him with his goats in tow, and hoping, at the same time, that I would eventually find the camp. It was ridiculous. He probably knew that as well.

The flat rocks beside us had dried out by now. I sat on one of them, my rifle pointing down. I placed my helmet on another. He picked, as his seat, a rock opposite mine and handed me a piece of pita bread that he pulled from his side pouch. That was followed by an offer for milk.

"No, thank you." These were my first words. I was not yet used to goat's milk. Later, in my tank unit, I had the opportunity to acquire a taste for it.

The Shepherd

My next words were, "Listen, I have no intention of reporting you . . . In fact, I am lost."

His eyes smiled in amusement and became even brighter. "You know," he said, "I have a son your age, he is also a shepherd." I started to wonder how many shepherds cohabited with the army on these mountains.

He then added, slowly, "I know where your camp is. I have been running up and down these mountains since I was a child. Would you like me to guide you?"

"Yes, that would help a lot."

We must have walked no more than ten minutes when we arrived at a point overlooking a valley. Down below were row after row of small, two-man tents adjacent to the bigger, communal tents. He pointed down and said: "There is your home. I must go on now."

We faced one another. He really was a part of this mountain. This mountain was also a part of a military range. We had to train hard after so many wars.

We wished each other good health and went our own ways. I saw him disappear among the trees and shrubs, followed by his small flock of goats.

My problems were not over. I looked at the vegetation around and, within minutes, made use of the camouflage techniques I had learnt only the day before, turning myself into an odd-looking tree. I'm sure I looked rather peculiar sneaking my way down the hill, hopping from rocks, to trees, to rocks, walking low or crawling. It actually did not take long. They were not big mountains.

Just as I snuck into the back of my tent, after clearing all vegetation from my body, I heard my unit come out from the dining room tent. They had just had breakfast. The flap from my little tent opened. When he saw me, David, my tent buddy, was stunned and relieved. My first question to him was: "Has anyone noticed that I was missing?"

His answer was: "I am the only one; we went straight from training to breakfast. Where have you been for four hours? I was scared stiff!" I quickly explained, but omitted the role of the shepherd. David's reaction was funny:" You slept! Do you have any idea of what we have been through in the meantime?"

I could only guess . . . I quickly changed into a dry uniform. That day we had a horrendous day and evening of training, but no night exercise. Our officers knew what excessive sleep deprivation could do to new soldiers. Over time, we learned to sleep standing up.

I ended up with the one a.m. watch. My mind went right back to the top of the mountain as I turned my back to the camp and gazed into the dark, steep hills engulfed in a blue light. There was a half moon crowning the mountain range.

I could distinguish the trees and some of the bigger rocks. I wondered where the shepherd slept at night.

A week later, as a bus was taking us on our expected short leave, I felt a deep sense of gratitude for the man who had given me the most precious gift a soldier can receive. A day of normalcy, love, good sleep . . . back home. I figured that the army had known for a long time about the shepherds. This wise shepherd knew about young men. He had tactfully helped me back on my way.

On this occasion, I was really the only one who had been in trouble. For many years, this had been grazing land and somehow continued to be except when used for military training. This shepherd was at home. I was a guest. I smiled and promptly fell asleep.

Claude Weil

Joan Baez ~ The Power of Song

I had known for a while that tanks can cry.

I was numb with cold. This was the last night watch. A sad winter light slowly outlined the contours of the white buildings around me. My hands were frozen on my Uzi. I was not a happy soldier.

What a miserable, forlorn place this tank base was in the dead of winter! Years of armour training by generations of soldiers had left the area desolate – not a square metre of grass, and I cannot recall ever seeing trees. Nevertheless, I would rather sleep in tents out there than bunk in those decrepit buildings dating back to the British mandate. Two of these buildings sheltered our unit during training. At night we froze on the bunk beds. There were no glass panes in the windows. Military buildings are ugly. They confine the view and the mind.

Even the ground was repulsive . . . a fine powder with little sharp rocks, not the greener fields of central Israel or the golden sands of the Sinai. Training had always been hard and intense, testing the limits of our endurance, but it took place mostly in natural settings, away from anything built by men. I loved that.

Earlier on, during boot camp, I had found out that the Negev was also a rocky desert. A cut to the hand or knees often meant an infection. I thought that nothing could be tougher, more demanding than the infantry training in the Negev. I was wrong. The Negev displayed beautiful, rolling hills and deep *wadis*[4]. There were also

4 *Wadi* is the Arabic term traditionally referring to a valley. In this case, it refers to a dry *riverbed* that contains water only during times of heavy rain. The speed at which water may flow suddenly into a *wadi* makes it a dangerous place when upstream and sudden rainfall occurs.

Joan Baez – The Power of Song

mountains of red rocks. I will never forget when we climbed one of these mountains on our knees with a man on a stretcher because we broke the rule of absolute silence the sergeant had ordered. If we made the slightest sound or dropped the stretcher, we had to climb the mountain again. Even the water bottle had to be completely full or empty, to prevent any sound. The threats worked – we succeeded in climbing up and down the mountain like ants and we walked the ten kilometres back to camp, eleven men taking turns carrying a fellow soldier on that stretcher.

While in the Negev, every evening a third of the unit was on an intravenous diet because insufficient supplies reached our camp due to some administrative error, as explained by our captain. We were on perhaps 2,000 calories a day rather than the 4,000 to 5,000 required. We became malnourished. Others were sitting with their feet in metal ammunition boxes containing an antiseptic solution to combat infections. Our bodies were taking a beating. However, bodies heal from infections and twisted ankles. Here, in this godforsaken Armoured Corps training base, it was our spirits that were under siege; a much more serious condition.

In twenty minutes, another guard and I would wake up our comrades. They would curse us as we shook them hard and pried them away from pleasant dreams. Some begged for another two minutes in the sleeping bags before swapping, in seconds, their white long johns and t-shirts for their uniforms. That is how cold it was. Mornings were for theoretical training in tank technology and warfare. Afternoons and nights were for field training.

But now, to add to the early morning gloomy atmosphere, the eleven tanks decided to cry. Was it the warming morning air condensing on the cold, massive metal bodies? They simply cried. How do you console a tank? Their tears rolled down the vertical armour; droplets fell on the dusty, thirsty ground.

However, I had a shield to protect me from the morning blues. Folded in my coat pocket were letters from my mother and Betty, which I had already read countless times that night. They were covered with tank grease, but the love and warmth they radiated conquered this gray, dismal dawn. That worked until I made a serious mistake.

A few weeks before, Betty had given me her small transistor radio before going back to Canada. I decided to turn it on, close to my ear, to ease the last minutes of night watch. I could not have hit a more formidable obstacle. The warm and thoughtful voice of Joan Baez filled the air and my soul. She sang her version of "Suzanne," a song written by Leonard Cohen.

Against this, I was helpless. The words spilled from the radio, my shield incapable of defending me.

On this cold February morning, in a remote, Spartan Israeli Defence Force's Armoured Corps base, do you know, Joan Baez, that you made eleven tanks and a tanker cry?

Claude Weil

The Flower and the Tanker

At noon in the rolling sand dunes of the Sinai Desert, the sun becomes a white-hot, shining ball of fire that overheats human, animal, and machine.

It was the spring of 1977. I was an "old," accomplished, fully trained tanker. Indeed . . . I was twenty-three.

We sat in three tanks, A, B, and C, barrelling at high speed through low dunes and flat, sandy plains, slicing through the sweltering air. We had already spent hundreds of days and nights in this desert, which had begun to feel like home. I felt at peace in this wilderness, despite the arduous tasks involved in manning the tank. It is a land disconnected from the petty worries of life. As Jewish Berbers, my mother's family had spent 600 years in the Algerian desert plateaus, so deserts resonate in my blood.

This region is vast, arid, and unforgiving, but it can be tamed and can become an almost sensual escape once you learn to mould your habits to its many facets. Whether in a nerve-wracking sandstorm or under the glistening warm summer nights where American and Russian satellites chase each other in a dense background of stars, the desert in its rich emptiness is a comfortable home to me.

The sounds of the tanks were disturbing in this setting, but there we were. I was sitting on my little white metal seat with the paint fraying at the edges, after hours of early morning training that had stretched, as usual, until noon and would take us to midnight. Inside the tank, a world of shells and my foldable Uzi submachine gun were securely latched onto the walls of the dreaded metal machine. The sounds of tank tracks, sometime combined with the vibration of the ground, is enough to instill fear in most reasonable humans.

I had, many months ago, learned my craft and the necessary reflexes that would prevent my head from getting caught in the

The Flower and the Tanker

massive breech of the main gun, incessantly swinging up and down under the control of a gyroscope.

I also learned to move in tandem with the rotating floor so I wouldn't get caught against the static lower part of the circular turret while the floor and the upper part of the turret rotated. I was an experienced tanker.

In fact, despite the heaving body beneath me and the enormous roar of the diesel engine at my back, I was in the midst of a rare peaceful moment. In one of the deep pockets of my combat suit, I had five letters from Betty tucked away safely. I had received them the previous evening all at once.

She wrote to me almost daily from the serene library of York University in Toronto and could not know that there was only so much the military mail service could accomplish.

Every Thursday, often late at night, I would routinely receive a pack of five letters when I returned from the field. This brought broad smiles to the faces of my fellow tankers. By now, the latest quintet was blackened with oil and smelled of diesel and cordite.

But I had them, and that was enough. I knew that soon we would take a lunch break, and I would rest my back against one of the tank's bogeys and shift my body until it was cradled in the hot sand, pull out the letters, and read them for the third time.

I wondered how many times one could eat Chinese takeout at university, for a moment forgetting my daily fare of cucumbers and tomatoes. Everything in those letters and cards was dainty, from the delicate illustrations to Betty's rounded penmanship full of passion and tenderness.

I was so engrossed in my daydream, I did not even bother peering through the periscopes and episcopes surrounding me, even though we were riding all hatches closed and at the ready. All in all, I was a happy soldier.

That was when it happened.

My radio set came alive with swift orders. We were quickly grinding to a halt. In a fraction of a second, the letters were forgotten and the entire crew became alert and sharp like a pack of hunting wolves.

What could be next? Would I load the shell? Start the fans? A year of training was kicking in. I was one with my machine, as much as I had been moments before with my Betty. Only now I was void of thought, prepared for action. Gone was the young woman in the library at York University.

I was now back with my fellow combatants, back to being an element in a shield no one was allowed to breach . . . somewhere that day, in the Sinai.

When the order came, it was surprisingly brief.

"Disembark now. Something has happened to Tank C."

We quickly jumped from the turret, carrying our Uzis. These belonged to the tanker, not the tank, and had to be carried at all times when operating outside. While all the hatches of tanks A and B were open and the two crews had disembarked, we could see three crew members of tank C, exiting visibly shaken and holding their heads.

The tank had abruptly ground to a jarring stop, over the distance of a few short meters. No one had ordered such a brutal manoeuvre, which had resulted in the turret crew's banging their heads on the thick, hard, metal surfaces.

There were no serious injuries, but there was astonishment all round.

Tank operations followed carefully choreographed manoeuvres orchestrated by clear and firm orders. Why had Mario, the driver of Tank C, abruptly stopped the machine he had so entirely mastered? It could only be due to a serious situation in the driver's compartment, located in the front left of the unforgiving contraption.

Mario was the only one still sealed inside the machine, the hatch above his head locked. By then we had all formed a half-circle in front of that hatch, and waited for a minute that felt like an hour for a sign from Mario.

Suddenly, in the complete silence of the desert, a harsh click was heard – the hatch popped open a few centimetres and slowly rotated. At first all we saw were Mario's two very large hands – those marvellous hands found on Italian artists that had produced masterpieces such as Michelangelo's *David.*

Indeed, Mario was a tall, wholly handsome soldier of Italian descent. He had a square face with strong, Roman features and intense green eyes beneath a shock of tight, reddish-brown curls.

He extracted himself from his compartment, his lanky body and wide shoulders unfolding until he was fully erect. He did not say a word, just looked at us intensely and then finally opted to plop himself off the tank.

His gaze was on fire, but had an undertone of sadness and lurking despair. Even our lieutenant, who would normally have requested an immediate explanation, had been stunned into silence by his stare.

Slowly, Mario bowed his shining head towards the ground and simultaneously spread his arms out, extending his palms upward. His gaze and the direction of his hands met at a point in the sand.

We all, as one, looked down, following the silent directions he was giving us – and there it was.

A lone flower, its petals a vibrant purple against the harsh yellow of the sand, had grown from a seed that had after many years found the few drops of dew necessary for it to produce a live plant of simple beauty.

Twelve pairs of eyes were gazing at this short, fragile, light green stem and delicate crown of petals. Finally, the deafening silence was broken by Mario's deep voice. The vibrant green of his eyes was glistening with unshed tears, his voice thick as he uttered: "I can't anymore."

The reality of what had happened dawned on us; our hearts tight, our stomachs queasy, we simply looked at him, our gazes alternating between his eyes and the innocence of those petals.

Mario had abruptly stopped his fifty-ton machine to avoid crushing the flower. He was no longer a tanker, and had made the instant decision that he could not mask any further the reality of his profound humanity.

The lieutenant gently asked Mario if he would agree to drive his machine back to the camp. He nodded in agreement.

After many months of intense training and unimaginable strain, this was by far our toughest test. None of us had spoken a word. I recall putting my hand on Mario's shoulder for a few seconds. His eyes caught mine briefly; I had never seen such desperation in the eyes of another since boot camp.

It was a long thirty minutes to camp; we really did not know how to handle what had just happened. We knew it was forbidden to leave a space in which the mind of a soldier was not occupied; otherwise doubt would tear us apart.

Late that evening, Mario was summoned to the officers' tent. We sat at the edge of our flimsy beds, sitting in the sand, in tents shared by eight crew members.

An hour later, Mario returned to us and we surrounded him; something wonderful had happened. He would never climb into a tank again.

He had placed an offer on the table before the officers and it had been accepted. He badly wanted to stay with us and did not want to be sent to some store management job, cut away from the eleven crews that had become his family. At his request, Mario would become a key player in the kitchen tent. This filled us with joy; we would not lose our brother.

Mario had at times operated the kitchen when our cook was on leave and knew how to turn the most ordinary ingredients into the finest cuisine.

From that day on, in our corner of the Sinai, we got used to the regular visits of the non-commissioned officers and officers who would take long detours from their paths to taste Mario's legendary Italian cooking.

For about nine months, in the gruelling heat and under the infinite cover of stars, Mario dutifully made it a point to never leave the kitchen until the last crew member was back in the dead of night; and he served his comrades meals that only the rich and famous could afford.

For a brief moment in history, Mario's kitchen became the most defended Italian restaurant on Earth. At the backs of our minds, the wonderful scent of scaloppini was our bridge to all those we had left behind, while operating in that land cut off from all other lands.

Raouf Omar

The Lady from Bat Yam

I was sixteen or perhaps seventeen years old and still in school. As usual, I was working. I needed to support myself and my family. It was a hot summer—one of those you always talk about years later: "I remember," you say; "I remember that summer of nineteen-something-or-other . . . G-d, that was a hot summer . . . record heat . . ." and on and on.

Yes, it was one of those summers, and I needed to work to save for school. Fate answered my call. One day one of my neighbours in the Balata camp took me with him to find something to do.

At the time, Palestinians from the West Bank would head somewhere into Israel—anywhere in Israel, when we could still go there, to find a job for the day, the week, or the month.

Most would go to a city somewhere between Jaffa and Tel Aviv—the name escapes me now, years on, but we would go to this city and crowd into the city square, where we would wait to be picked by contractors for one day's work or more.

My neighbour, Abu Mohammed, took me with him and managed to get me a job with an Israeli contractor who went by the name of Abu Salim. He spoke Arabic very well, with a Jaffa accent, since he lived in the Palestinian community there.

After introductions, Abu Salim urged me into his car and drove me to the job site, which was in a small city south of Tel Aviv called Bat Yam.

We drove to another city square, an open space with a massive hole in the ground. Beside it was an even bigger pile of sand. Abu Salim bluntly told me to fill it in. Abruptly, he handed me the tools I needed and told me he would be back at five p.m. to pick me up and take me back to the city where I could meet my neighbour and return to Balata. Of course, Palestinians were not allowed to sleep overnight in Israel without permission. With that, he waddled back to his car and drove off, leaving me there in the heat of the early morning sun to do the job.

Beginning at seven a.m., back and forth, back and forth I worked, barely pausing to wipe my sweating brow. It was back-breaking work, but I kept time by watching the progress of the ball of fire overhead as it crossed the sky. In the late afternoon, I looked up and saw that the sun was disappearing on the horizon. I had worked all day with no food or water. I could tell that five p.m. had come and gone, and I started to panic.

I had no money and no permission to stay in Israel past sundown. I waited . . . and I waited . . . the cover of dark soon enveloped me in that little town. I was young, alone, famished, thirsty, and terrified.

I left everything and I started walking . . . walking until I arrived at a row of houses nearby. I picked a door and I gathered up whatever courage I had left to combat my fear and I knocked.

A lady of around forty-five or fifty answered the door and stood quietly looking at the strange, dusty, Arab kid standing, shaking, at her door. In my broken Hebrew I managed to explain what had happened. Understanding came slowly to her face, and she nodded. I was blessed for the first time that day, it seemed, in the shape of a kind-faced Israeli woman: she knew Abu Salim, since he was the area's contractor.

Ordering me into her house, she gave me a large glass of ice water and told me to sit at her dining table while she went about finding where Abu Salim lived. I watched her in awe, this small woman talking quickly into her phone, too fast for me to catch what she was saying; but I was thankful to rest for the short while.

Soon, triumphantly, she told me she had found out where he lived. For the third time that day, I got into another car to be driven somewhere new. We arrived at his house, and the determined woman pounded on his door. A young girl, perhaps his daughter, opened the door and was subjected to a barrage of Hebrew asking where her father was. As Abu Salim walked to the door, I stared at this woman. No one had shown such anger on my behalf before. She yelled and screamed at Abu Salim, who stood like a young boy caught with his hand in the cookie jar. In her swift Hebrew, she demanded to know how he could leave a kid alone like that, with no money, food, or water for the whole day and fail to show up!

The Lady from Bat Yam

I remember understanding some of her words and her saying: "If you don't pay him *now* I will call the police and file a complaint against you!"

I stood watching in awe of her, waiting for him to call her bluff. *File a complaint over a Palestinian kid?* I thought to myself. *She would probably get laughed at!*

But Abu quietly shuffled off to his office. He came back with my wages plus overtime. I took the money from him and quickly followed her back to her car, without another word.

It was around nine p.m., and I couldn't make it back to my camp that night. There was no transportation left. The woman drove me to a motel in Jaffa and told me to stay the night there. It was a known hotel, illegal, really; mostly Palestinians stayed there. I thanked her repeatedly, but she just shook off my thanks and waved me into the motel.

I didn't sleep a wink that night, my thoughts alternating between terror that the Israeli police would raid the hotel and wonder over the actions of a Jewish-Israeli woman supporting me. *I was important in her eyes. I had value.*

Sometime around dawn, I drifted off to sleep for about an hour. Around six a.m., after rubbing the grit from my eyes, I made my way home to the West Bank. It was another day. I would soon have to find another job across the Green Line.

Claude Weil

Celebration at Sunset

As a soldier on duty during a seemingly everlasting conflict, I reached for deeper, richer, spiritual resources to connect with my small family. Bodies may be separated, but with the spirit's force, souls can meet across long distances and periods of time. I found it easier to do that under the radiant and soft energy of the Holy Land's stunning sunsets. They helped me disassociate from whatever reality I was currently in and connect to the universe's infinite power, where I could travel at will. I was a free man. Meanwhile, I carried on soldiering, while at each sunset my soul would travel on another journey. The following are some of those journeys.

In June of 1977, when our first son, Raphael, was born, I was given a short leave to be present at his birth. That evening, Garry, a Vietnam veteran, played the guitar and sang the blues for the entire kibbutz, improvising a moving song to celebrate Raphael's birth . . . I still have the tape of that memorable, soft, warm, evening.

My captain had insisted on being told when the birth was likely to happen, as he wanted to come to the kibbutz to celebrate with us and be a witness of a possible *Brit Mila,*[5] should the new baby be a boy. I tried to reach him through a long line of military connections from Naharia, in northern Israel, to our camp in the Sinai. A handful of young women soldiers in charge of communication, through a chain of military bases, were excited by the news that a fellow young soldier had become a father and feverishly worked the telephones. They were unsuccessful in making the connection with our unit near the town of Yamit and Kibbutz Nir Itsahk. I guess it was just too far out . . .

They, too, had dreams of being mothers someday. Meanwhile, they went out of their way in trying to be like women free of their

---

5 Ritual circumcision.

uniforms. They shortened their skirts and opened the top buttons of their shirts until an officer would lose patience with them and command them to dress appropriately.

I returned to my unit with my hands full of cartons of cigarettes and two bottles of sweet brandy. Meir, my captain, a lanky, red-haired and dedicated officer, was disappointed at not having been able to attend the circumcision. However, he forgave me when he realized that I had tried hard to have him contacted.

He quickly improvised a spontaneous military-style celebration. One of the dining tent tables was moved to the middle of the square formed by the tents and eleven tanks. Food and military issue plastic cups were laid out on the table. The forty-four crew members joined in, still in their dusty gear, as they had manned the tanks all day.

Meir stood before us, and behind him, to the west, was the most glorious sunset that the Sinai could offer. There was a sphere of melted gold, with delicate spokes of light red, slowly sinking into the brown sand as the luminous moon discreetly emerged from the horizon. The desert, sun, and moon had decided to join the party with a display of magical beauty. These sunsets freed us from the constraints of daily concerns.

Meir lifted his cup and started to speak. His emotions were palpable, his voice kind yet firm: "Soldiers, a baby boy was just born in the land of Israel, may G-d bless him and his parents. It is a celebration for us, as we must remember that our work here is that of creating the conditions for a lasting peace so that, maybe, one day our men and women will be able to remain close to their newborns and never be forced into shelters. We have a new soul to protect. As I speak he is probably sleeping in the baby house of Kibbutz Sasa as we prepare for our night training. He and his mother count on our strength, skills, and determination. Claude cannot be with them, but he can protect them. That little boy has brought us joy, and may G-d bless his soul. Let us raise our glasses to Raphael . . . *l' Chaim*!"

By then the unit was engulfed in a warm sphere of soft, red sunlight, a gentle hand cradling the crews in their dusty uniforms and tired bodies. It was surreal. Stars had started twinkling in the infinite, dark blue sky. How small our cluster of humanity must have looked, all dressed alike, from the vast galaxy expanding above us. Yet how serious our challenge was, down here, our feet constrained by tall leather shoes.

The birth of Raphael brought a moment of peace and tranquillity, a salve to the souls of forty-four young men separated from the world and attached to the umbilical cords of eleven heavy machines, the sole purpose of which was to destroy life.

I was lucky; I had found some salvation, a sense of redemption from the insanity of it all. I was now more than a soldier. A part of me that until now had lain dormant in my mind blossomed, just as seeds in a *wadi* wait sometimes for years for life-giving rainfall that turns them into fields of flowers displaying the most delicate colours. On such days, crowds of people swarm from the North to share in this awesome display, one of nature's spiritual masterpieces – the desert in bloom. Time can be a great healer as well as an architect of beauty.

When the short celebration was over, and the crews headed for the dining-room tent before the night's training, friendly hands vigorously slapped my shoulders and back. I was numb. All that had happened appeared to unfold in slow motion. The suntanned, cracked faces of my fellow comrades radiated warmth and simple joy. Others were more solemn. My gunner, Shimon, a strong, handsome, dark-skinned Iraqi Jew, for some reason unshaven, displayed a broad, happy smile. His bright, shiny eyes and smile were amplified by the evening light, etched in his prickly, jovial face.

The intensity of the moment overcame me. I then remembered that a few months earlier, Shimon had saved my life. As I was trying to un-jam a machine gun while the tank was moving fast on an undulating piece of desert, my head had become trapped between the gun breech and the turret ceiling. This machine gun had to be brought back to life, and I was being punished for having removed the safety shield. My microphone was twisted and I could not be heard. As a result of my convoluted posture, I was out of reach of the flat, bright red emergency release switch that could prevent my head from being crushed. This is when Shimon turned his head towards me, his face lit by the dimmed red turret lights. His eyes opened wider, but he remained calm like a sphinx, a tanker through and through. He quickly corrected the angle of the main gun with his electric controls and freed me from imminent death. I sat dazed on my little white seat, but managed to inform the crew that I would be "out of this conflict"

Celebration at Sunset

for a few minutes. I was bleeding from the left cheek. My glasses were bent out of shape. I fixed them, breathed deeply a few times and returned to action; the training had kicked in, as self-pity was a luxury we could not afford.

On this luminescent evening, my flashback was a stark reminder that birth and death are inextricably interwoven. Shlomi, a lanky, thoughtful soldier from another crew, approached me: “Maybe your son will not have to be in a tank—you know, like us.”

As Shlomi walked ahead of me into the dining-room tent, with his characteristic long and dragging steps, I noticed the discreet zipped pocket we all had in the upper back of our combat suits. It contained a handle used by rescuers to pull a crewman, or his remains, through the narrow hatches of a dead tank. Our planet is so vast, so beautiful, nothing wrong could happen to us. Shlomi would never be pulled out of his tank that way . . . right?

To this day, I see forty-four boys, their faces reflecting mixed emotions, lifting their cups of cherry brandy to celebrate my son’s birth, the sun, moon, and desert dancing a slow tango to remind us that one day it would all end. But what would other sunsets bring?

Claude Weil

War

Some sunsets melt into the night and carry with them one's uneventful day, sending it into oblivion. Some move the soul . . . for a moment. And then there are those rare sunsets that change lives and lift the soul into the spiritual, the unforgettable, and the eternal. I call them spiritual storms, as they have the same awesome force of sandstorms capable of moving massive dunes across long distances.

One such spiritual storm had occurred when my unit celebrated the birth of my son; for a few moments, hardened soldiers became angels.

Another started early one morning when we were told to prepare to go to war in Lebanon – Operation Litani – in 1978. The tanks were loaded on the flatbed trucks. Yonatan, an immigrant from the UK, and I were actually about two kilometres from where the action was taking place. We were on a separate mission away from our respective tanks and had to wait for a jeep to pick us up. We sat in an empty camp, a twin of ours, with a bunker full of ammunition, patiently waiting for some tanks to arrive with a batch of new "special" trainees.

What a contrast with the previous evening, when we ate a feast of a meal: pickles, goat's milk, and canned beans cooked on a fire sustained by transmission oil, lit with powder and a spark from a battery. When you have no matches, you improvise. The goat's milk came from passing Bedouins who traded it for our endless supply of pickles. It had been warm and fresh, direct from the goat's udders.

Now, from our vantage point, the yellow morning sun was playing games with the large camouflage nets our comrades were placing on the tanks. It was another surreal moment. I sat on a cot and tried to listen to some music on my small transistor radio. It did not help, as I felt myself disconnecting from the world of normality and from my memories. All the pieces that comprised my life's jigsaw puzzle separated and vanished no matter how hard I tried to visualize the gentle faces of Betty and Raphael. Something had taken their place, a theatre of bleak, Spartan reality whose dancers could only be the crews stretching nets over their machines like a well-choreographed ballet. My training had taken over during this fearful, ominous dawn.

Our tanks never left the southern front. Reservists from the Northern Army eventually carried the brunt of the operation meant to stop the incessant shelling of *katioushot*[6] on Israel's northern communities. These rockets hurt Jewish and Arab Israelis alike.

Ironically, I ended up on my kibbutz in charge of security together with a handful of men. Betty and Raphael were in France. There was an increased risk of terrorist attacks in times like these, so I carried an ugly magnum handgun at my side for a few days. Our instructions were to storm immediately any building, such as a classroom, that may have been overrun. Losses, including innocent children, were expected on both sides. Waiting had been proven to only increase the number of casualties.

I so missed the desert. There, only soldiers fought and died. Now the war straddled the border between Israel and Lebanon. On both sides many innocent civilians were confined to deep shelters. Children were sometimes born in these shelters.

In the evening, at around seven p.m., large reservist artillery units stopped by our kibbutz to regroup, eat, and call their families. I will never forget the moment I watched a forty-five-year-old reservist with long, red, curly hair, his powerful forehead glistening with sweat, and his large frame silhouetted by a red sunset. He was talking calmly on the phone to his teenage daughter and wife. She could not see the hundreds of soldiers and colossal mobile artillery vehicles standing at a stone's throw from her husband. Yet he gently spoke the most soothing of words to his loved ones, his M16 hanging by his side.

There was a dispute between his wife and his daughter. In less than three hours, he would be in combat, yet he gently tried to find

---

6 The plural, in Hebrew, for *katiousha*. It is a short-range or mid-range rocket shot alone or in groups; originally a World War Two Russian weapon. It exists in various calibres. Simplified versions of it can be manufactured in small tool shops.

War

the words to appease both of them. Anxiety had invaded his home. It would show its ugly face in many homes on both sides of the border – even more so where the innocents resided.

I had to ask him to let other soldiers use the phone. He looked at me briefly, hanging up the phone, noticing that, despite my civilian clothing, I was also a soldier. I was armed and had a military haircut.

So many fronts had to be protected. Far to the south, in a hangar, my tank was waiting for me and my crew just in case things heated up on the southern front. In the turret, there were four bags loaded with our gear, our names on them.

Sadly, perhaps, I remained calm and efficient. We had kibbutz families to protect, other convoys to assist. I helped to organize the lines around the telephones and the large pots of soup until the night patrols started. On a regular basis, the artillery crews climbed onto their long, heavy, war machines, parked on the nearby road, and left in columns as others came in.

Around ten p.m., I watched from the roof of our archeological museum the dim blue lights at the rear of those serpentine convoys driving along the border and then cutting into Lebanon. The long-range artillery fire started in complete darkness. Now massive shells were crossing paths with *katioushot*, which had terrorized Northern Israel. On both sides, long flashes brought terror to villages and olive fields alike. The cycle of violence was on again.

All this was happening not far from the place where Adam and Eve strolled in the Garden of Eden; that snake had gotten more than it had bargained for.

My walkie-talkie came alive; the patrols had to be efficient and well rehearsed, with a war raging in the background and families sleeping in shelters on both sides of the border.

In the morning, Druze gardeners from a nearby village came to work with Yehudit, a founding kibbutz member in charge of covering the kibbutz with flowers. I loved these Druze gardeners, their dignified postures, their immaculate white *kofeya*[7] and their deep blue eyes. At lunch they would open up a large one-layered pita containing goat cheese and green grapes, which they ate, unrushed, under an olive tree. Their people had witnessed so much history. They knew better.

7 A headdress.

The shelling had stopped. I pushed open the door of our tiny apartment, fell into bed, and slept for a few hours. Most of the men I worked with in the apple orchards were absent, having been mobilized. Around noon, I drove a lone tractor down to the fields and tended to the young trees until the next night patrols. I was alone and surrounded by 50,000 apple trees of all sizes and varieties. These orchards, on rolling hills, were a splendid sight. Why can different trees coexist—even complement each other—when people have so much difficulty doing the same?

That previous sunset had been one of doom; people had died, and anything I could write will never adequately convey its effect upon me. Mercifully, soon after, a young Palestinian woman would bring a strong message of hope to my scarred soul, one soft evening, at the beach.

Claude Weil

By the Sea

A wave. . . it emerges from a mass of water, assumes a perfect shape crowned with white foam, rolls for a while, and dies on the beach. Its life is short, an expression of natural beauty. The sea was scintillating under yellow, red, and purple strata, sinking slowly into the horizon. I was at the edge of a beach, in Tel Aviv, sitting on a bench. It had been a long day, and as much as the waves were in perfect balance with the grand scheme of our planet, I was out of balance with it. The city was hot and stuffy in comparison to the dry desert I loved, and far too crowded. So I stayed right there on my bench by the shore, as the salty wind cooled my burning body, and wave after wave slowly soothed the nostalgia that had crept in unnoticed.

I was back with my crew and our tank, carrying out for a few days a mission that may still be classified, on a naval base located at the corner of a trendy, popular beach. What a contrast we made, during the day, with the sunbathers and their families. Only a thin, tall, concrete wall separated us. Our tank's screaming engine, running at high rpm, was at odds with the flow of music coming from hundreds of transistor radios. When I stood on top of the turret, I could see men and women wearing skimpy swimming suits, drinking pop, and eating just about anything one can buy or bring to the beach. I had no complaints. I did not envy them their world, as I felt I was serving a higher purpose.

Behind us, the sea danced its slow tango.

Every evening around seven p.m., we received one hundred Israeli pounds, a lot of money for a soldier and a kibbutznik, to cover our expenses for the nightly leave in Tel Aviv. We were expected to be back early in the morning. I had absolutely no use for this money. I did not even have a wallet. I spent my nights with Shimon and Assia, delightful people and relatives of Betty's. I had no intention of sitting

By the Sea

in a café, on a stuffy and humid night, wearing my uniform and with my angular Uzi on my lap. I felt most comfortable in the desert or in my kibbutz. I still feel this way and have walked in many deserts.

I was much too far from Sasa to be able to hitchhike my way to Betty and Raphael and be back on time the following morning. This was my reality. Other crew members were luckier and made their way home nightly.

This particular evening, I needed the sea and the dying sun as companions. There were too many symbols of civilian life around me, a continual reminder of my small family that I could not be with. So, my Uzi over my shoulder, my bag beside me, I sat quietly and let the sea appease me.

I was starting to recover my underlying strength when a determined female voice interrupted my meditative mood.

A thin young woman was sitting just metres away, holding the knotty fingers of her grandfather's hand. It took me a while to realize that he was blind. He wore a light jacket over a long, narrow *kombaz*,[8] and a *kofeya*. His face was turned towards the sea, guided by the gentle surge of the waves.

So here was an Israeli soldier and two Palestinians bathing in the calm and softness of day's end, a short distance away from the noisy, pulsating city.

"There are not many married soldiers your age. I am Leila; what is your name?"

My wedding ring, shining in the sunlight, had attracted her attention. Indeed, very few conscripted soldiers are married.

The young woman was talking to me. I turned towards her. She had very delicate features framed by shoulder-length, thick, shiny black hair. She wore Western clothing, but her dress ended well below her knees. Her grandfather had not reacted to her intrusion. She had his blessing. He must have known she could handle any situation with maturity, pride, and wisdom and must have had an important reason to talk to me. He never uttered one word, but I felt he talked to her through the contact of their hands.

She must have been eighteen. I was twenty-three. I was stunned, as Palestinian women did not often address Israeli soldiers in that manner. I said nothing, which prompted her to keep on talking to me.

8 A white gown.

"So, you have no name . . . If you are married, how come you're sitting here and not going home? Your wife is waiting. Soon I will be married, and my husband will come home at this time. I will cook for him."

To see a lone married man at family time had shocked her. I had to say something: "I am Chaim (my Hebrew name), and I cannot go home. I do not live in Tel Aviv."

"Where is home?" she asked bluntly.

There was no messing around with this assertive young woman. "'B' Tsafon [meaning 'in the north']."

"Your wife must be sad and lonely."

Now I had a problem on my hands. A soldier is supposed to reassure the population, by being stoic and not letting his feelings show too much with civilians. Yet, that evening she must have intuitively sensed my thoughts and noticed the shadow of loneliness on my face. So I decided there was no point in displaying a false sense of bravado. "I am sure she is . . ."

"You are sad, too, I can see it. You must be a good husband. When are you going to see her . . . next Shabbat?"

"I do not know when I will see her . . . and my son."

"What do you mean? You have a son!" She became quite agitated and her hand left that of her grandfather.

"We have a baby boy."

At that very moment, she crossed her arms, placing one hand over her stomach and the other on her bosom . . . her eyes became teary.

She composed herself and placed her hand back on her grandfather's.

"Enough of that! Enough of that!" She meant enough of this endless conflict and the damage it did to people. She wanted a family; she wanted peace for her family, and her empathy for me, my pain, had triggered a primal reflex in her.

"My children will see their father every day!"

At that moment, her grandfather, who probably had heard enough, tenderly pulled her hand. They stood up and left quietly. They took a few steps, she paused and turned around one last time, a child walking sideways alongside her grandfather. Her gaze revealed not only compassion but also fear for her own future.

I remained for a long time on my bench. Only metres away, behind a wall, a tank was resting in the sand, its engine and exhaust manifold still hot. Hours north, a young woman and a baby were playing together, while here another young woman was walking her blind grandfather home, with anxiety tearing her mind apart.

In spite of our differences, she had understood me, captured my feelings, that of a husband and father longing for his loved ones. Her tears glistening in the waning light were imprinted on my mind. She had suddenly realized that, just like me, separation and incertitude may be part of her future life as a wife and mother. I wondered: If peace ever came to the Holy Land, would it be women who would finally negotiate it?

The Telescope

Raouf Omar

The Telescope

I do not remember exactly, but I believe it was 1969 when I met David. He was French, Jewish, and had moved from France with the hope of making his fortune in the Promised Land.

He was well built: not too tall, not too short, and red. He had red hair, a red face, and sported a large, red beard that, to me, made him appear still redder. However, even more striking were his eyes. They were laughing eyes, eyes that conveyed a sense of joy and delight in all that they gazed upon. With his multicoloured motorbike, large helmet, and ruddy appearance, he seemed to me, a young refugee from Camp Balata, to be an alien from outer space in love with his motorbike.

My older brother, Saki, and David were working together on a construction site in Natanya. He had invited David to visit us in Balata. Together they had arrived on David's motorbike. Saki introduced him to my family. I liked him immediately, especially his laughing eyes and warm, genuine smile. Intuitively, I knew I was safe with him.

David was astonished by the cramped, simple, living conditions of Balata, devoid of any luxury. The narrow streets were full of children. In an effort to bring joy into our lives and overcome the desolation of the camp, we Palestinians had large families. During the day, Balata was filled with a cacophony of the sounds of human activity as people called out their wares, or their ability and ingenuity to repair whatever was broken. Our large families had to be supported one way or another, and the constant hustle and bustle was evidence of this. Evening was the opposite: far too quiet. David was amazed at the difference; at how calm and tranquil it became.

We had a simple, traditional dinner and spent most of the night talking. David stayed overnight, and we awoke at about four-thirty the following morning, greeted by crowing roosters. Every family had roosters and chickens. It was an economic necessity; they did not take much effort in return for the bounty they provided.

It was time for the two of them to return to the all-important construction site. Competition for scarce employment opportunities was intense, and punctuality was of paramount importance. Money also meant additional opportunities for our family. Saki would be riding to work on David's motorbike.

That is when I heard a cry of despair from David. What had happened for David to behave in such a manner? I went over to investigate and saw David in a panic. He and his bike were inseparable, and it had disappeared from in front of our home. I imagined he believed it had already been broken down into spare parts for the local entrepreneurs. I began to laugh, tears rolling down my face. David's expression was questioning. "Why are you laughing?" His eyes shouted at me: "Don't you realize what has happened?"

With a big grin on my face, I answered his unspoken question: "I'll get it back for you." You see, I knew who had taken it. It was not difficult for me to figure out.

I scurried out of the house and collected some of my friends along the way. I knew every street, every alley. Nothing could escape me. I also knew all the small, innocent gangs of children who roamed the area. It was easy for me to quickly locate the bike. A group of kids had taken the motorbike to play with. For them it was an exciting new toy! They were eager to have fun with it. Together, my friends and I wheeled it back to the house. There was not a single scratch on it. The look of immense relief on David's face was quickly replaced by a magnificent smile and those wonderful, laughing eyes. I was elated for both of them. He thanked me repeatedly, profusely. It was as if I had saved his life. With a joyful wave, he and my brother took off for work.

The following week, David returned. He had brought me a present, a telescope. "This is for you," he stated simply. I was surprised, but delighted with the unexpected gift. He continued: "You are a good kid, you have a vision for your life. You will be successful, and of this I have no doubt."

I believed he had been astonished by the night sky on his previous visit. Our house, sheltering seven, had no electricity and consisted of only two rooms, just like all the others surrounding ours. In the summer, everyone slept outside, in the open. There was nothing to impede the spectacular, clear, jet-black sky. It had inspired him to give me the telescope. Of this I was certain.

I thanked him and told him I would guard his motorbike every time he visited, but I had no words to adequately express how I really felt. He had made me feel much older than my age, but even more important, I realized that so-called enemies could coexist and overcome their pain.

I loved that telescope. As I stared towards the heavens, there were no boundaries to my imagination; all dreams were possible. The telescope is still in my family home in Palestine. Now, when I look at the night sky, wherever I am, I often think of David . . . the warm-hearted red Frenchman.

Claude Weil

From Man to Child

From Man

It had started quite innocently, as I was on a short leave, with the drone of an engine coming from the south. A small yellow plane flew a gracious curve while dispersing leaflets over our kibbutz on the hill. I plucked one that had come to rest on a rose bush and carefully read the coded information written on it; row after row of passwords. I was recalled. I ran to our small apartment and informed my wife, Betty, of the leaflets, put on a uniform, and grabbed my Uzi and side-pack. I stepped out. Gone were the blue shorts, light summer shirt and sandals. I was a tanker again. I had changed worlds like a feline moving from peaceful rest to an alert, hunting posture in seconds. The most aggravating factor was that my mother was visiting from France and was completely overwhelmed. I had never been recalled in that way.

Now, in a lost corner between the Sinai and the Negev, I was half deaf from three days and nights of incessant shooting at a wide array of targets, fixed and moving. My back was sore from the uninterrupted loading of shells. I peered from my hatch before night darkened the entire landscape. I had never seen so many units from all the services, regrouped for what could only be a major show of force involving the bulk of the southern army.

A crackle from the radio was followed by an order to stop the tank, but we remained inside the turret, all hatches closed. My mind slowly drifted to the incident that happened just before we had joined other units for these massive manoeuvres.

In our area of the camp, hundreds of men had lined up in two parallel columns winding their way to the polling stations. This was election time. As per Israeli tradition, both slow-moving columns, cooking in the sun, argued about the merits of one party over another. Yitzhak Rabin represented the Left and Menachem Begin, the Right. We argued respectfully but with passion. Our hands did most of the talking. We needed a prime minister who could conduct meaningful negotiations leading, step by step, to a lasting peace with our neighbouring countries. Who wants war forever?

By early morning the following day, as I was finishing the last watch, I found out on my little transistor radio that Menachem Begin had been elected. I ran to our tent and yelled the outcome of the election to my sleeping comrades. The orthodox crews were from the Right, the other half of the crews were from the Left. I never saw soldiers wake up so fast and enter into such heated arguments that came, suddenly, to an abrupt halt. All the soldiers, sitting on the corner of their beds, wore sombre expressions accompanied by a deafening silence. The clamour, followed by that sudden silence, had attracted the attention of our captain, Oren. He entered our long tent and stood like a rock.

Dan, an Israeli-born soldier, had been heard telling an immigrant soldier, Yossi, that if he did not like the choice of Menachem Begin, he could go back to his home country. Dan had committed what the army considered to be a very serious offence. Yossi, an immigrant with no other family in the country, had been humiliated, diminished as if there were two classes of citizens. I was such an immigrant and felt the bite.

No one spoke . . . then the orthodox soldier who had uttered the insult stood up and, with some references to G-d and the Ten Commandments, admitted his comment had been inappropriate and apologized. His words clearly showed regret and distress. The knot in my stomach became less painful. On the other hand, the captain's facial expression, always so stoic, had turned into a mask of tension, anger, and disappointment. This had happened in his unit, amongst crews that were supposed to be like the fingers of one hand: "Yossi, Dan, go by the flagpole and talk for a while, and then Dan will be charged." I sensed that Oren had a plan. He was made of steel, but was also very wise.

Twenty minutes later, the unit lined up outside near the flag, in full uniform, armed and impeccable, facing a sergeant. Oren came forward and, as usual, did not say a word for a long time. His look went slowly along each row, observing one soldier at a time with piercing eyes that went right to the far reaches of our consciences. This was unbearable. My body was one tense muscle.

We felt some relief when Yossi asked for permission to speak. "My Captain, Dan's parents are immigrants from Yemen. He is in great turmoil and showed humility when he apologized to me. He is ready to face the consequences of his act. I have accepted his apology. My Captain, I am respectfully requesting that no charges be pressed against Dan."

Another long silence followed the request. Finally, in a firm but calm voice, the captain spoke. "You have trained hard for the honour to replace your fellow tankers who perished during the Yom Kippur War. What happened today should be considered a disgrace for the entire unit, starting with me. However, the words I heard from your comrade indicate that this unit has not lost its cohesiveness, integrity, and honour. Now prepare for one of the most difficult periods of training you have ever experienced."

This was an understatement . . .

As our tank was ordered to rejoin a larger force of hundreds of other tanks and infantry carriers, the roar of the monstrous diesel engine abruptly brought me back to the reality of the dim red light in the turret. It was so dark outside . . . Running over our own infantry was a gut-wrenching worry. This is when things went wrong.

First, the gunners and loaders of three tank crews, including ours, disembarked to help our captain's tank get out of a deep crater. It was a nightmarish scene of towing cables, stretched to their limit, taut, ready to snap and slice into our fragile human flesh. I remember vividly being afraid. I had no control over the situation; a cable might snap or it might not. Our uniforms were white with dust. We had turned into ghosts.

Incidents throughout the night culminated with our tank's being hit by friendly fire. We managed to continue as the driver diverted fuel from a damaged external reservoir.

To Child

By early morning, our platoon of three tanks came to a halt in a location we could never find again. Hatches were opened and ghost after ghost emerged from the massive machines. Never had twelve

From Man to Child

crew members looked so inhuman. Our faces had turned into tense masks with sand plastered around our eyes, noses, ears, and lips. One of our lateral fuel tanks had been split wide open by a mortar hit, but the diesel fuel had not caught fire, just spilled out. It was a disturbing sight, yet we were too exhausted to truly care.

Our tanks, sitting at awkward angles on overlapping dunes and with guns pointing in every direction must have been a hellish sight.

This is when it happened.

Shlomi was the first one to notice them: "Look up there!" We focused our eyes to the top of a small dune, right above our heads. The rising orange sun lit two little Bedouin boys holding hands. One, the older, perhaps six years old, wore blue shorts. His little brother had red shorts. Their skin was a light brown and they had very dark, smooth hair. Their tent could not have been far away.

I felt terrible. We were such a worrisome and awful sight. They were a surreal vision enhanced by the golden sand and sun. Surprisingly, they did not seem afraid. Although shy, they observed us with curiosity and intensity. This is when our somewhat overweight young driver lost it and shouted: "Go away, leave this place." He was perhaps twelve years older than the two of them and was holding a round, bright red, clock radio. Its dial was adorned with an image of Mickey Mouse. This situation was too much for him to bear.

Shlomi turned around and pushed him hard. He fell in the sand, on his back, stunned, the clock on his stomach.

At that moment, as one, crews opened the side canisters of our tanks. The sharp click of the latches was deafening. They loaded my arms and those of Shlomi with loaves of bread, cans of jam, and sweet pickles. We climbed up the dune, slowly, speaking kind words to the two boys who stood motionless having not moved a single inch. They accepted our gifts, their faces alternating between soft smiles and sombre facial expressions. We carefully balanced the loads on their tiny, brown arms.

The two young Bedouins waited until Shlomi and I returned to our tank, then swivelled around and disappeared. This is the last we saw of them. We helped our driver get up, apologized, but otherwise remained silent. The space the two little boys had once occupied was now inhabited by a dazzling orange light. I wondered if this had been a dream, but the open canisters on the tanks proved otherwise. There is so much strength in the innocence of childhood. It had allowed us to show our true nature.

The tension in our minds was slowly replaced by a fragile feeling of joy and renewal. As my vision interplayed with the infinite blue sky, I dozed lying in the sand. I was exhausted.

An hour later, the lead tank radio came alive; it was calling us back to action. The dune on which the two little Bedouins were standing was now a harsh yellow. Today, when I face the dishonest, the greedy, or the violent, I remember the morning when there were three tanks at our backs and two angels above us.

Raouf Omar

The Boxing Match

It was the summer of 1969 on a beach in Gaza. With soft sand underfoot, and warm, gentle breezes caressing both body and soul, my cousin and I walked, ran, and splashed among the waves of the Mediterranean, her hair flying unencumbered in the breeze. To me, this woman was the embodiment of all that nature's canvas could portray. Her complexion was dark, and she had long, black, lustrous hair, impossibly long eyelashes, jet-black eyes, full, generous lips, and an engaging smile capable of disarming the most hardened of souls. We were in love. Unable to speak of it to one another, we communicated through the holding of hands and the look in our eyes. Silence was golden. The summer was idyllic, peaceful, and perfect.

Following the 1967 occupation, Palestinians in the West Bank and Gaza were finally able to visit each other. My mother was visiting her sister who lived in Alshate Camp in Gaza. We stayed for five glorious days; my cousin and I spent most of our time at the beach. Compared to the crowded conditions of Balata, the wide expanse and freedom of the beach was a rare opportunity. At the end of my family's visit, my cousin promised to come and visit me in Balata in two weeks' time. Although I was sad to leave, I had to rush back to study for the National Final Exams. High marks would guarantee my admission to university, a cherished dream that I had worked consistently hard to achieve. My love for my cousin was an even greater motivator; I would finish university and then return to her.

My cousin's family visited us as promised. I told my mother I wanted to marry her. Mother approved, giving me her blessing. However, she added: "You are still young. It is important to go to university and complete your studies first. This way you will have a more prosperous life for yourself and for your future family." I agreed. I studied diligently day and night and succeeded in obtaining one of the highest marks among all the students in the West Bank in the National Final Exams. I was going to university!

However, life does not always allow you to follow your dreams. The Occupation not only fragmented families, but also relationships. Even though our dream was unfulfilled, I was driven by the strength of her love to succeed. I believe that the best love in one's life is eternal love, as it is pure and sustains hope. Today, my love for my cousin continues to be a driving force in my success.

After returning to Balata from our visit to Gaza, I focused entirely on my studies. In Balata, I was a member of their soccer team. Playing sports, in addition to the competitive aspect, was a means to combat boredom, stay out of trouble, and maintain a high level of fitness. This had been important to me from an early age. Our team had a "Physical Training Club for Youth," one of the few places in Balata that had electricity. I had a key to the club and frequently would go and study there through the night, as we had neither electricity nor tables to sit at in my house.

The club was situated on the edge of Balata, next to the main street leading to Nablus. Every night, as I studied, I would look out the windows and see the Israelis, in their jeeps, patrolling the road. I'm sure they often wondered why the coal black of night was pierced by light from the club's windows. Electricity was a rare and precious commodity in Balata. One night, a jeep stopped in front of the club and four soldiers entered. Another one, the driver, remained in the car. Their berets identified them as officers. They wore green uniforms; their Uzis hung from their shoulders, pointing down to the ground, their hands resting on them. Two spoke Arabic to one another. They greeted the three of us studying there that night: "Salaam."

I was standing in front of them with an open book in my hands. Sometimes I liked to walk around the room, rather than sit, as it helped me to memorize information better. "Can I help you?" I asked the senior officer, a large man, who was standing directly in front of me.

He answered me with a question: "Why do you have the lights on? It's after one a.m."

I explained that the three of us were studying for our exams here at the club because it had electricity and tables, which our houses did not have. We often would study through the night, I said, drinking tea

The Boxing Match

to help keep us awake. He seemed reassured, but I was uncertain and I asked him: "Would you like some tea?" Strangely enough, he accepted and sat down at a table.

He asked casually: "Are you sure you are not doing anything else?"

"No," I replied. "You have the freedom to check the club if you want." One of the other officers checked all the rooms and returned with a big smile on his face, saying: "Everything is fine except for these." He held out a pair of boxing gloves. The seated officer laughed out loud as they all continued to drink their tea. We chatted about the club's sports activities.

"Who boxes?" asked the senior officer.

"I do. I also wrestle," I replied.

"How about having a boxing match with me?" he asked.

"No, no I can't afford to injure myself. I have to be ready for my exams. I need to do really well if I am to be accepted by a university."

He insisted and I reluctantly agreed, but with one condition.

"What is it?" he asked

"I want you to put down your weapons and take off your berets. I will only box against a man, not a soldier." They all agreed. To me, this was of paramount importance, as it signified that we had become equal, not men on opposite sides of the ongoing conflict. I was very fit, fast-moving, while he was a little slower. The bout went back and forth for about five minutes with no one having a clear advantage. I knew I could wear him down over a prolonged period of time, defeating him, but I kept thinking of how I could end it without embarrassing him in front of his fellow officers. I wanted to get back to studying. I decided to give him an opportunity to hit me. I pretended I was hurt and fell down, holding my jaw. He started laughing, stretched out his arm, and pulled me up. At that moment, the driver outside honked his horn, signalling the officers that it was time to leave. He grabbed his Uzi, put on his beret, lit a cigarette, and turned to leave.

At the door of the club, with the cigarette hanging from the corner of his mouth, he looked directly at me with a large smile on his face, that smile revealing that he knew I had thrown the fight . . . I had let him win. I smiled back.

Claude Weil

The Sandstorm

Our crew was sitting in a light truck. Our usual tank commander had been replaced by a reservist for some reason unknown to us. Also, sitting quietly on one of the two benches was a female lieutenant. She was athletic in stature with short, black hair tucked under her cap. She was also very pretty. In Israel, interracial couples often gave birth to stunningly beautiful children. Her shoulder patch indicated she belonged to the medical corps. Her name was Hanna.

My throat was as dry as a *wadi*. We were heading southwest, straight across the Sinai, following a flatbed transport carrying our tank. A unit of young recruits, on improved American Patton M48 tanks, was being field-trained, and we were going to be their opposition, "the enemy." Our tanks were Russian T55 Tirans, refitted with 105mm guns, Browning machine guns, and infrared night vision capability. As such, they were called Tiran 2. These tanks were left behind, sometimes damaged, by the Syrians and Egyptians during the Six Day War of 1967. The unit of trainees needed to be able to identify the silhouette of the enemy.

We came to a halt in the middle of a cluster of white buildings probably dating from the time of the Turkish Empire. This was a crossroad that I would never have been able to find on a map. The flatbed truck carrying our tank had also stopped.

As we stepped out of our vehicle, I looked around. This was a barren spot, a kind of "last stop before nature takes completely over from humans." A tent beside a flag post sheltered a few reservists. There was a small food outlet, as well as a shoe polisher, who also sold trinkets. Both Arab men needed our business. I had a warm orange juice and a dry chicken sandwich. It really was the last stop in the vast desert.

The Sandstorm

As I was kicking the dust waiting for my friends, I drifted towards the shoe polisher. I could not give him an age. He was dressed all in white, his tanned head covered with a small, round hat. He immediately asked me to sit for a polish. I politely declined, simply because my grandfather had told us many years ago: "Boys, in this family, we polish our own shoes." He had applied this principle in Algeria, although he was a great friend of the Arab population. Furthermore, in the Israeli army at that time, we polished our shoes but never shined them. Excessive shining was too symbolic of the German army's style during World War Two.

I observed the shoe polisher's reaction. He was very disappointed. I could not explain my rationale. He pointed at his house and his children, who were running and playing, but he remained very dignified. He refused the few *lirot*[9] I was willing to give him. He wanted to apply his craft. I had no right to rob him of his dignity, so I sat and let him polish my shoes, short of the shining.

He accepted his payment and spoke the following words: "You are a decent man, so I will tell you something that will help you for the rest of your journey south. A sandstorm is coming."

I realized that, as a man of the desert, his ability to read the sky was second nature and far more developed than mine or that of my companions. This was his world and he knew its many gifts and dangers. I looked far away, towards the horizon, and noticed a faint yellow colouration rising in puffy columns assuming the shape of a tormented cloud. I thanked him. I reported the information to my comrades; the driver peered at the horizon with a pair of binoculars and simply said: "Climb in the truck . . . *now*." He was going to attempt to outrun the oncoming fury. Cutting off twenty minutes from the remaining three-hour ride could make a big difference between making it to the unit or not. Otherwise, we could be stranded for days at this crossroad in a tent with our fellow soldiers and our acting tank commander, a reservist who was to be released in two days. As we climbed onto the back of our truck, I turned towards the man in white. He was walking back to his home. Hanna, the lieutenant, remained serene as she was climbing back into the truck. For the first time, I realized she had huge inner strength.

---

9 Plural in Hebrew for *lira*, equivalent to a British pound.

The threat of the oncoming sandstorm reminded me of a sad story involving another sandstorm . . . it was about six months earlier. We were on top of one of the Judean hills near Beit Shemesh, training with elements of the Jerusalem Brigade or a related unit. Lumbering up the steep hills at sunset was a strain for the crews of the three tanks. We had been told of the existence of a deep cave on the way up. It was getting dark, and no one was sure of the location of the cave. All of that was forgotten when we reached the top. To the east, Jerusalem was aflame from the setting sun. It was truly a breathtaking sight! The magnificence of the moment was soon disturbed by the rumble of older-model half-tracks joining us. One by one, they lined up in close proximity to our tanks. I guess liaising with us was the end of an exercise for a segment of this unit.

Sitting in the half-tracks were many men, some pot-bellied. I felt a deep emotion as I realized that they were all over the age of fifty. These men had served for a long time – about seven years as conscripts and reservists in peacetime and war. That made them veterans of the 1956, 1967, and 1973 wars. The dignified way in which they sat, the way they held their M16s straight with the butt on the floor, the properly buttoned shirts, all were signs that they had remained dedicated, capable soldiers. We were facing history wrapped in courage. Later, as we talked together, we found out that some of them still had pieces of shrapnel in their bodies.

We sat on top of our turrets, not knowing what to do or what else to say. These hardened soldiers could have told us, with bravado, that we still had a lot of learning to do. The opposite happened; they looked at us with infinite kindness. One pulled out a box of pears and started to throw them to the crews of each tank – enough for us twelve boys.

Then I finally understood. We were of the ages of some of their sons and daughters. They cared about us, as, perhaps in one of their last roles as reservists, they were probably passing the torch to us. I am sure they would have liked to have achieved peace. Now they would grow old with the knowledge that their children would be fighting wars to keep this country safe until, finally, the peace that had evaded them would flourish. Their service would never end. Worry would replace action.

I jumped from my tank and stood by the first half-track. The soldiers spoke kind words while at the same time pretending to have an interest in our tanks, perhaps to preserve our young egos. One of the veterans, quieter than the others, said to me: "Beware of sandstorms."

"What's with sandstorms? I am more concerned with being hit by a rocket if we go to war . . ."

Within a minute, my face was red with shame as he answered me: "As we speak, Tanker, my wife is probably sitting beside Rivka, our daughter, by the beach in Natanya. Rivka was an officer . . . She was serving in a forward medical unit when her vehicle overturned during a sandstorm. She will spend the rest of her life as a diminished single woman."

I lowered my head, my fingers, like claws, pressing very hard on the armour of the half-track. This veteran was dying a slow death from grief, having not been able to protect his daughter from the unforeseeable.

A jolt of our truck brought me back to the reality of the infinite Sinai and the sandstorm chasing our truck. I was told we were close to our destination. As we arrived around six p.m. at the field unit, every tent was shuddering with its flaps swinging in every direction. I looked up towards the north. The sky was glowing from the setting sun, outlining a giant, brownish wave with long, rounded fingers with puffy rings reaching out to us. The shoe polisher certainly had it right. A major sandstorm would arrive any minute and we had little time to prepare for it.

The captain of the Patton unit greeted us. We all knew there would be no training for at least two days.

The trainees were doing a weekly maintenance on their tanks and equipment. Every shell and some tools were sitting in the sand beside their tanks, some on tarps, some not. Our first instinct was to warn them, to yell at them: "Don't you see? Pack your shells and equipment; seal your tanks!" We had done that the minute our tank was unloaded, sealing machine-gun ports and sliding a hood on the main gun.

Their captain, anticipating our reactions, asked us not to say a thing. His recruits needed to learn . . . He would stay with them right through each phase of the storm. Sand was now mixed with the air we breathed, and a concert of particles, hurting metal and tents, rose quickly into a deafening crescendo, denser and denser.

By then, we were an odd microcosm in a single tent—a truck driver, a tank crew, and a medical officer who was serenely observing what was happening around her. We had hoarded food and water in our tightly sealed tent. The tank commander was not happy. He was going to serve past the end of his reserve period. His family and job would have to wait. Sandstorms can last for days. They move enormous dunes from one side of a road to the other, altering the landscape. Rapidly the relentless wind and hammering of the sand particles, mixed with dust, jars the nerves. The sandstorm envelops you in a tense fog of anxiety. It cuts you off from the rest of the world. Each pillar of sand is a bar of the jail.

I peeked outside through a small opening in the tent flap. The tanks' floodlights showed bent silhouettes trying to dig shells and equipment out of the accumulating sand. This was a hopeless task that could only be completed after the storm. Each of us took turns peering through the opening. Some shook their heads. One, the truck driver, said: "Poor beggars."

We turned away from Hanna to let her undress. Preserving one's dignity is always on the mind of a field soldier. She laughed and told us to relax. She had been given the opportunity to sleep in another tent, probably with officers.

She wore essentially the same military underwear as us.

We settled in our sleeping bags. The tank commander started to curse in the dark at the storm that would delay his release from reserve duties. We started to tease him. He had been recently discharged and had a date with his sweetheart that he probably would not make.

All this time, Hanna remained silent. I wondered about her and finally asked: "What will you be doing here?"

"I am a military psychologist. We are concerned about some recruits who are showing signs of distress. I am also here to assess the overall well-being of this unit—and, by the way, you guys are fine. It is the quiet ones we are concerned about."

I so understood what she meant; we had lost a friend to a horrible suicide during boot camp. A psychiatrist had been sent to our unit. By then we were in tank training. When he came to our tent, housing eight crew members, we took turns telling him how miserable we were, hoping for a leave. Meanwhile, he could see cards on a bed, open books, a game of Monopoly, letters . . . and, quite frankly, we were tanned, fit, and very healthy.

He stayed for a while and finally said: “It is the quiet ones I am looking for.” These were almost the same words that Hanna had uttered.

Then we started to laugh. He laughed, too: “Sorry, guys, good try!” and he moved on to the next tent.

Back to the present, we woke up early but stayed in our sleeping bags for a while.

We had to brave the sandstorm to go to the “toilets,” essentially holes in the ground in a wooden shelter, sometimes with a plank to sit on. There were huge scarabs trying to climb up the sandy walls of these pits. During our boot camp, the shelter and the plank were omitted during field training.

The showers and outdoor sinks were clogged with sand. One of us stayed near the “toilet” while Hanna used it. A soldier could have showed up at any time. Watching the showers and toilets for female staffers or visitors was something we all had routinely done. We viewed the lone female soldier in our brigade as a mother figure. Our mothers were what we needed in our semi-permanent state of exhaustion, separated from our families. This is the way it was.

The storm lasted another day. The young recruits had been allowed to stay in their tents most of that day. We spent most of the time lying down, chatting, reading on our beds, drifting into reveries, or gazing at the top of the tent’s pyramidal roof.

By four p.m. the next day, the storm was over. The trainees were removing ten to twenty centimetres of sand from their shells and equipment, depending on what the pattern of the dying winds had been. Often the wind that brought the sand was replaced by another wind that took it away. From eight p.m. until the next morning, we trained with them. They had a more advanced rangefinder than ours in their later version of the M48. They were disappointed when the “enemy” tank scored much better than they did at long-range shooting.

During the debriefing, their captain told them that within a year they would match our scores or do better. This was accurate. The training makes up for small technological advances. We were seasoned tankers. They would be, soon.

In the afternoon we left, returning the way we came. Hanna stayed behind. She had yet to meet some of the trainees.

The reservist was two days late and would miss his date. I noticed that a gigantic dune had crossed the smooth roadway. It was now opposite a road sign I remembered rather than alongside it.

I also wondered where on this road Rivka, the daughter of the grieving reservist, had become disabled. The Sinai could be unforgiving in peace or in war.

When we stopped at the cluster of white buildings, I approached the shoe polisher and sat on his chair without being asked. "You were good to me and my friends. This was a strong sandstorm," I said. He smiled at me and replied: "Today is much better." In the powerful Sinai, full of surprises, we had developed a connection. To the north, the sky was a solid blue.

Raouf Omar

Conflict at the Bus Station

It was a hot summer, and I was eighteen or nineteen years old. It's difficult to be precise, as time has a way of clouding one's memory. What I do know is, the Holy Land was in a state of uneasy calm. Although there were no direct, prolonged periods of protracted hostilities at that time, no one was immune from frequent, random acts of violence. Heightened awareness was the norm – part of a regular day.

I had finished work for the day at a wholesale store and was walking to the "Tahana Merkhazit," the central bus station of Tel Aviv. It was an enjoyable thirty-minute walk. I loved the daily opportunity it gave me to indulge not only in people-watching but also in looking into the varied stores. To me it was both relaxing and entertaining, as well as a means of keeping up with the fashions, despite the fact they were considered to be those of the enemy. Anyway, I felt safe, with no irritation except from the armed civilian or uniformed officers who, traveling in pairs, would always stop you. I never liked their questioning and repeated requests for identification; it felt strange, but I never became angry; I was used to it.

Arriving at the bus station, I noticed a large crowd had gathered and could hear loud screams coming from their midst. Ever curious, I had to know and see what was going on. I managed to push my way through the Jewish crowd and witnessed a fight taking place. Two Jewish men, both bus drivers, were punching one another, although it was evident one was clearly outmatched. Apparently there had been a driving incident. One driver was young, tall, and very muscular, while the other was much older, shorter, and fat with a large, protruding belly. The latter's energy was spent, and the young man began hammering powerful blows onto his face. The old man was teetering, his face bleeding profusely.

Conflict at the Bus Station

The crowd had now formed a circle, but nobody attempted to intervene and try to do something to help the injured man. I don't know if they were enjoying it or were afraid to offer some form of assistance . . . but I was angry, very angry that nothing was being done to halt the fight. I clearly remember him doubled over clinging to the younger man's shirt and receiving non-stop blows to his head, face, and stomach. Pity for him surged through my body and, without thinking, I found myself sandwiched between the two drivers and then splitting them apart. I don't know if some bystanders were ashamed, embarrassed or insulted by a Palestinian boy's intervention, but I noticed that many were relieved to see the altercation come to an end. In our culture, it is a tradition to get involved when two men are fighting and to separate them. I pushed the victor to his bus and then took the other to his. I sat with him, calmed him down, and offered him a coffee. We chatted for a short while, but I had to leave, as I did not want to miss the last bus home.

After that time, whenever either one of us was at the bus station, we would always look for one another and we would stop, chat, and always have a coffee together. His name was Jacob, and he was a sincere and kind man. Over time, in spite of our ages and cultural differences, we became friends.

For almost two years, we continued our friendship. One day I asked him a question that was of great importance to me. I had been thinking about it for a long time. "Is it not a shame that my ancestors and parents used to live very close to this spot where we sit and now I am a Palestinian who needs a permit to visit or work here?"

Jacob started to laugh and said, "Leave the subject alone, as we cannot solve it. Our solution is for the two of us to co-operate and be friends. If this happens among all Jews and Palestinians, we will paralyze the politicians and put them in order." He continued: "Look, you care about my family; I care about your family; and if that expands all over the Holy Land, we will finally have peace."

I replied: "This is the hope that I – and most people – believe in and should work towards."

We lost touch with each other when I moved back to Lebanon to finish my university studies. I don't know what happened to him, but I hope he is still alive; he is probably in his late sixties now, and I hope that he has a chance to read this book. I remember on one of the

Jewish religious holidays, Pesach, he gave me a bottle of wine and a large box of chocolates. Today, when I see a box of chocolates I often think of him, a good friend. I wish him and his family well and hope we can meet again one day and be surrounded by peace in this tragic and wonderful land.

Claude Weil

The Tanker and the Bedouin

I have always had a deep sense of respect for the proud Bedouins of the Sinai and Negev deserts. They inhabit a vast region, from the western coast of the Sahara, through the Sinai, the Negev, and ending with the Arabian Desert.

Bedouins' connection to nature and its many expressions is profoundly grounded in spirituality. Bedouins can read the land and the sky like an open book. They know well before anyone else that a sandstorm is coming and never lose their way. When a visitor arrives at their camp, they have sensed the upcoming visit for hours. Do they know something we don't? Have thousands of years of frugal life in the vast open spaces created a special bond between the Bedouins and their creator . . . our creator?

One crisp dawn in 1976, on my way to my unit, I had the privilege to observe the camel-mounted Bedouin unit getting ready for a deep desert patrol. There was no sight more beautiful than seeing these men of the desert, wearing large capes, a black or blue veil partially covering their dark skin and even darker hair, rise simultaneously on their camels, which were covered with brightly coloured blankets. A rare cluster of palm trees in this compound added to the magic of the moment, giving it the feel of an oasis.

According to a timeless ritual, they formed a caravan that was going to travel for days visiting Bedouin camps, settling disputes, liaising with Israeli health and welfare services, administering justice, keeping an eye on the infinite landscape of dunes, and checking the precious water resupply points.

Shortly after, another soldier, Hanan, and I had an opportunity to volunteer to ride in a truck to Beersheba, a desert city, to help the driver pick up and load cases of shells and machine-gun ammunition. It was like a mini-vacation, a welcome break from the incessant and relentless training.

Once the task was completed, we realized that since only two could sit in the truck's cabin, one of us would be stranded. In the event of a rollover, the soldier riding in the back, sitting beside those heavy crates, had a very limited chance of coming out alive. I eagerly volunteered to be the stranded one in Beersheba for a mini-leave. I would hitchhike back to our camp, located well south of Rafah. The driver would inform my captain.

We were just following regulations – until I felt the urge to "walk light." I did not give Hanan much choice: I placed my Uzi on top of his lap as he sat in the truck's cabin. I asked him to place it inside the wooden ammunition crate beside my bed upon his return to camp.

I had just broken a sacred rule. A combat soldier and his weapon are never to be separated. There was real danger to be faced on the way back. The unit was located in hostile territory, not far from the Gaza Strip.

Both Hanan and the driver shook their heads in dismay. What was happening to the soldier that they knew for his seriousness and even temperament?

Soldiers often hold back their stress and inner wounds until an event or opportunity triggers a release. This explains how, weeks earlier, some of us had stripped at dusk and had run naked into the Red Sea, as female soldiers were guiding us on an educational trip and our officers were away. True enough, we did not have swimsuits and we used camouflage techniques so as not to offend anyone. Yet our guides were not amused as a group of tourists, mostly young women, applauded the sight of tankers swimming in the nude! How good it was for us to feel ten years old and carefree. We were in need of some form of purification. The sea does this to soldiers; it calls them and they willingly surrender.

Now, I pretended to be a tourist in Beersheba for a couple of hours. I strolled along wide, large, neatly landscaped walkways ornamented with palm trees and flower beds. I savoured the flowers' penetrating fragrances. It appeased me. I walked through the market and I drowned myself in the scents of the countless exotic spices displayed on trays or large burlap bags. I gobbled a falafel, and then,

The Tanker and the Bedouin

glancing at my watch, in a matter of seconds I became a soldier again. I guess I never really stopped being one. It was time to hitchhike my way to camp. My escape was over. I had peered at life through a very small window.

I asked my last ride to drop me off at a dirt crossroad about five kilometres from the unit. Having no weapon, I would have to cut through the desert and sneak my way back into our camp.

A while later, I came upon two Bedouin tents silhouetted in the spectacular desert sunset. They were shaped like the wings of bats and located about three hundred metres apart.

As I was walking between the two camps, an enormous, snarling German shepherd darted out of the western tent and in seconds was upon me. I began walking sideways like a crab and was removing my coat to fend off the attack. Suddenly, a woman dressed in black from head to toe gave one sharp call. The dog stopped on the spot. She stood straight, in complete control, the sun playing with her many gold bracelets. She did not utter a single word. I felt lost in time and space. She was the desert and it could easily have been two thousand years ago.

Through my evasive manoeuvres, I had ended up much closer to the second tent and suddenly exactly the same thing happened. A similar and even bigger dog had been stopped metres from me. Again, the mysterious silhouette of a woman in black contrasted with the sinking sun as the dog returned to his tent. I was so immersed in trying to somehow connect with the world I had accidentally stumbled on that I failed to notice, right beside me, a Bedouin man who, speaking in Hebrew, was greeting me. I was given some fresh water and sweet dates. He spoke gently, with some reference to the dogs. I thanked him for his kindness. As I left, I looked at him one last time. He truly was a splendid man of the desert with an innate, quiet strength. He represented a world halfway between ours and some other intensely spiritual space. I struggled, having accidentally stumbled onto that world, so simple, yet so profoundly rich.

Later that day, alone, I was sitting on top of my tank turret. I needed to reflect. The rolling, infinite desert was calming, like a caress. I was still confused about the recent events that had happened many kilometres north of the unit. There was a pink glow on the horizon, and, far away to the west, something or someone was moving. I felt the urge to enter the gunnery station to find what was this shape outlined by the sunset. Perhaps I already knew . . . I gripped the handles of the optical device designed to focus on a target. I was mesmerized, when I adjusted the sights, by the view of a kneeling Bedouin immersed in prayer. With a long, slow, fluid movement of arms and torso, he was one with the majestic landscape. I quickly withdrew from intruding on his privacy.

How could that be? Twice in the same day I had somehow become connected to men and women of this ancient people. Was there a reason? The events of the next day would confirm, at least in my eyes, that a message was being conveyed to our eleven crews, caught both in mind and body in a conflict unravelling in the land of the Bedouins.

Early the next morning, we climbed into our tanks, a long day of training ahead of us. First we had to align the main gun of each tank with the gunner's sights. We waited for a jeep with a checkered target to position itself a long distance away from the eleven guns. It was late, and our lieutenant was becoming impatient. He ordered all engines turned on to warm up the war machines. This is when he or a tank commander noticed a speck on the horizon. The order was received to assess if this could be a possible calibrating target.

Shimon, through his sights, quickly identified the "target" as a Bedouin in prayer. I became tense. It probably was the man I observed only hours earlier.

The radio communications within our tank were quite revealing. Tank commander: "Gunner, can you calibrate with the 'target' over there?" Shimon: "Negative, I need a proper calibrating target." Tank commander: "Understood." this was followed by a report to the lieutenant that I could not hear. Only our tank commander was in direct radio contact with our officer, so it was only later that I found out what had happened, based upon visual observations from my hatch and subsequent discussions with other crews.

Crew after crew quietly avoided pointing unloaded 105mm guns towards a praying man and waited for the proper checkered target. Yet, to the best of my understanding, this was done in a non-defiant way . . . discipline was maintained, reason and morality prevailed equally. Physically, we could take a lot; emotionally, too. But preserving our moral integrity was important to us, whether or not this was rooted in faith.

For many of us, prayer was a sacred pillar of strength. My own prayer was heard when, a few minutes later, the lieutenant ordered all engines down. There was a deafening silence throughout the row of war machines, until the jeep showed up. The calibration was executed to perfection. This day's training was harsh and efficiently carried out. A body-breaking tank charge was the culminating point. It is one of the most demanding and dangerous tasks for the crews, and a most horrifying sight for the enemy, as every action happens fast and at close range. It is not unlike hand-to-hand combat—with fifty-ton machines. Many crews in the Golan Heights had horrendous stories of just such moments in the opening days of the Yom Kippur War—if they survived this test of their courage.

In the Holy Land, the presence of a force, a form of energy lifting the soul, is frequently experienced regardless of time and place. That morning this force was embodied in the shape of a Bedouin with a solar aura.

At night, we drove back to camp, all hatches open under a wonderful dark blue, star-studded sky. As I took my turn guarding the camp, around two a.m., I was still very disturbed by the events of the past two days. What world had I run into? I stared at the glittering night and spoke humble words. Slowly, my weapon became lighter on my shoulder, my body warmed by an inner glow, as the stars reached out to me and formed a protective shell on the piece of sand I stood on. I was one with the force. The Bedouins had been my guides to the sacred.

Raouf Omar

The Police Officer

Jacob Smera, an Iraqi Jew, owned a wholesale store with his partner, another Iraqi Jew, named Fouad. Their store was located on a street in the Iraqi Quarter of Tel Aviv, where most of the stores were owned by Iraqi traders.

It was 1972, and I had been working in their store for a while. My job was to monitor all of the items coming into, as well as leaving, the store. I also delivered merchandise to the other Iraqi stores along the street.

Jacob, in his late sixties, was a tall man who had a disconcerting habit of using his tongue to play with his false teeth, moving them in and out and pushing them from side to side. He was generally angry in temperament and frequently in a bad mood. He always wore the same dirty old grey suit. He conducted his business in the same fashion he had done in Iraq. He sat behind his rough wooden desk surrounded by large, open, fifty-kilogram sacks of beans and grains, rarely moving from his chair other than to go to the washroom. There was virtually no free space in the dusty store, as the sacks took up all the room on the ground floor.

He was a man who rarely smiled or laughed. He rarely talked about his personal life. Sometimes, I could almost taste his anger and frustration about the rising inflation and missed annual holidays to Lebanon that he used to take from Iraq and that were now an impossibility, as he had become an Israeli. But he was straightforward, sincere, and honest. He had an exceptionally good heart, and I loved him like a grandfather. Fouad, on the other hand, I never liked. He was in his thirties, with eyes that were dark, insincere, and dishonest. I just could not look him in the eye.

I vividly recall an incident that further endeared me to Jacob. On one occasion, an old Yemeni Jew with a long beard, one of Jacob's business customers, asked him about the price of rice and some other grains. When Jacob replied, informing him that the prices had doubled compared to what they were two weeks earlier, he became very angry and used the Prophet Mohammed's name inappropriately. He didn't realize that I was Muslim, because they always called me "Raffi," and I also spoke Hebrew. I was gravely offended and asked him to leave the store. Imagine my surprise, when Jacob actually stood up! That was a rare event indeed, but the look on his face was unforgettable, one I had never witnessed before: pure rage and hatred.

"Hold on, Raffi," he managed to say to me as he flew across the room and grabbed the man by the front of his shirt, yanking him off his feet. "Listen, you bastard, Mohammed has nothing to do with inflation, and you are seriously insulting my employee, Raffi! I never want to see your face in my store again!" He raged. "I will never do business with you again! Never! Now get out."

Can you imagine this? He was defending me. He respected who I was and he was prepared to put his business on the line. My admiration for him knew no bounds. Jacob spent the rest of the day muttering under his breath while I worried that he was going to have a heart attack as a result of his intervention.

My mind flashed back to an earlier occasion when another Iraqi Jew had looked after my interests. His name was Abu. I had worked for him, briefly, prior to working for Jacob. Abu didn't have enough work to hire me full time and had personally recommended me to Jacob. However, one time, when I was doing some deliveries for him, he had said to me: "Raffi, due to inflation, the price of sugar will at least double, possibly triple, in two weeks' time. Why don't you buy three fifty-kilogram bags of sugar, and I will keep them here, at my store, and sell them for you later so you can make a personal profit?" I did. I actually bought four bags, one additional one for my family. That fourth bag worked out to be free, and I still made a handsome profit. I still hold Abu in high regard as a result.

In Jacob's store, there was a small staircase leading up to an attic crammed with boxes of canned goods. Here there was a small space with a chair where I would sit and have my lunch. Every day at around one p.m., I would see Fouad come up the stairs and shove the money from the day's sales under some boxes, to remain hidden until they could visit the bank, once a week, on Friday.

One morning, just before eight a.m., I arrived as usual just before they opened the store and wished them both "Good morning." Neither answered me. Both men avoided looking at me. "What is going on?" I asked Jacob. With a sad look he replied: "Soon you will know." I was nervous and wondered if I had done something wrong. It was difficult for me to keep my mind on my work.

At ten a.m., a man entered the store. He introduced himself as a police investigator and asked me: "Where is Raffi?"

"I am Raffi," I replied. He told me he had to speak with me. We went up to the attic. There he told me that there had been a complaint by the store owners. A large amount of money had been stolen. I was the primary suspect because I was the only one who knew where they hid their money.

"Look behind you," I said to him. "See all these stacks of boxes? Underneath here is where they hide their money. I have never dared touch it, as I'm very happy to work here, being with Jacob. He respects me and he pays me very well." The man nodded, gave me his business card with a time and date written on the back and told me to come and meet him at the police station as indicated.

The following day, I did as I had been instructed. The police investigator, an Egyptian Jew, spoke to me in Arabic once he realized I was Palestinian. I replied in Hebrew, explaining everything about the store in a comic manner, including my love for Jacob. He and three other officers who were listening in all laughed and became very relaxed as I told them my story. The investigator then took me to his office to talk some more before returning to the others.

Eventually, he told me I could go, as it was clear that I was not guilty of the theft. I explained to them that Fouad would fire me because he would think I was responsible. He said, "No, I'll provide you with a letter saying you are innocent." The other officers looked surprised, but they said nothing.

I returned to the store and gave the letter to Fouad to read out loud, because Jacob could not read Hebrew. The simple, but rare, smile that appeared on Jacob's face spoke volumes. He was happy, relieved that I was innocent, and he immediately told me to get back to work.

It turned out whoever had stolen the money had to have been much smaller in size than me. He had entered an extremely small,

The Police Officer

carefully broken window at the rear of the store. I had my suspicions that it was a close friend of my brother Joseph. His friend was a very small Jewish boy who often invited my brother to his house. I had seen him a few days after the robbery looking at the store from across the street. I had once told Joseph, who was three years younger than I, about Fouad hiding the money. If I could have proved it I would have told Jacob. As I stated earlier, I loved him like a grandfather and he deserved my loyalty and friendship. It would have been the very least I could do to repay him for all that he had done for me.

Why had the three officers looked surprised about the letter written on my behalf by the investigator? Apparently it was not customary procedure. During my conversation with the Egyptian police officer in his office I had told him I was studying at a university in Cairo and that I was working to pay for my studies. He made me Arabic coffee and told me to forget about the robbery. Instead, he talked to me about Cairo, where he had been born. Through our conversation, I realized I could trust this man. I relaxed; my studies would not be in jeopardy. He missed Cairo and had become somewhat melancholy, as he could no longer visit the city that he loved.

I told him, "You know, someday we may finally have peace. No more borders or checkpoints. Happiness would replace sadness." I offered to bring him back something from Egypt, but he said "no." It was then that we both realized something of far greater value and importance: we had become equals.

Raouf Omar

The Gramophone

I believe it was 1974. My brother, Joseph, was working in the well-established Tel Aviv neighbourhood called Karmel. It was a neighbourhood with many old houses. My brother had a contract with one of the families to remove all of the old tiles in their home and replace them with new ones. He hired me to work for him.

While we worked, we often heard loud music coming from somewhere outside. It was not just any music, but old Arabic songs that seemed out of character for the neighbourhood. I wondered out loud: "Who is playing this music?"

My brother replied: "Maybe it's an old Arab Jew missing the old days in his country of origin." My curiosity was aroused. At lunch hour, I said to my brother, "Let's go and check."

"Okay, let's go!"

Out we went, walking in the direction from which the music was coming. We followed the melody down a street and then turned into a very narrow alley. As we continued walking, the music became louder and louder. Eventually, we arrived at a tiny restaurant far down the alley. We stood listening for a moment, entranced by the sounds. Further enticed by the delicious aroma emanating from inside, we both entered.

A middle-aged man was standing behind a small counter serving traditional Arabic breakfast food: falafel, hummus, and *fool.*[10] He had thick, dark, greying hair, a small, neatly trimmed moustache, a dark complexion, and a jovial face. His broad smile displayed yellow-tinged teeth, indicating he was a heavy smoker. But what really caught my attention was an old gramophone with a large horn attached to it.

"So, this is what is playing the music," I said to myself. We introduced ourselves and he told us his name was Zelman and that

10 Fava beans.

yes, he was Jewish, and yes, he was originally from Egypt. We told him how enjoyable it was to hear music in a familiar language while we worked.

"I used to own a restaurant in Egypt and always played this kind of music. I continue to do so because it makes me feel like I never left home. This gramophone is all I have left from Egypt, along with this music."

He invited us for lunch, and we talked further. His food was wonderful, perhaps even better than our mother's cooking, but of course, we would not have told her that! He adamantly refused payment for the meal. We thanked him and told him that we would not return if he refused payment the next time. "Your music makes our work easier," we said to him. We returned to work, smiles on our faces.

At the end of every workday, we would catch a bus to take us to Tel Aviv's main bus station and from there we would take another bus to our home in Camp Balata. That day was no different, but our first bus ride was!

I remember that the bus was very crowded. Many passengers, including my brother and myself, had to stand up. Next to me was a Jewish girl about nineteen years old, with long blonde hair, and wearing a very short skirt. She was swaying from side to side. She looked at me with a big smile. I thought nothing of it until, with every movement of the bus, her body kept touching mine. She edged closer and closer to me. I felt uncomfortable.

Suddenly, she yelled out loudly to a man sitting in front of her: "Leave your seat!" Startled, he immediately complied. She pushed me onto the seat and, without any explanation, sat on my lap. I was nervous, scared, and I didn't know what to do. I could feel all the passengers' eyes on me; they must have thought I was her boyfriend. My brother laughed, but I was embarrassed. I didn't want any trouble as a result of her behaviour. I told my brother we had to leave the bus at the next stop. We did so, but so did she! Further embarrassed, I ran as fast as I could, while my brother quickly did the same, but still continued laughing.

The following day, back at work, we went for lunch at Zelman's. This time I brought him a present in return for his generosity: a modern machine for making falafels. One that was much better than

The Gramophone

his antiquated model, but difficult to find. However, in Balata it was available. He was ecstatic! He had wanted one for a long time but had been unable to find one. This time we insisted on paying for lunch. He reluctantly agreed.

I told him about the previous day's embarrassing incident on the bus and that I was scared to go back on that bus as the young woman might be there again. Both Joseph and Zelman laughed out loud. Despite their light-heartedness, I was worried about the possible negative consequences that her behaviour could create for me as a young Palestinian. "Don't worry about it," Zelman said. "When you have finished work, I will drive you to the main bus station."

From that time on, we developed a close relationship. We often invited Zelman to our house in Balata. He was single with no wife or children. Even after I left the Holy Land, he maintained a close relationship with my brother and my family. Whenever I look at falafel in my own restaurant here in Canada, I remember Zelman, his magical food, and the gramophone that led me to him.

Raouf Omar

Toppling Barriers

Before the first Intifada, one of our neighbours, Abu Mazen, worked as a gardener for an Israeli Jew inside the Green Line. Abu was a hard worker, punctual, reliable, and conscientious. These men were approximately the same age and had many common interests. Travelling daily from the West Bank, he established excellent relations with him. They held no hatred against each other and never discussed politics, knowing full well it would lead nowhere. This was a deliberate choice in a land where hatred was often the norm. They enjoyed many special times together, sharing meals and celebrations, becoming close friends, like brothers from the same family—a wonderful example of how friendship can overcome conflict and become a basis for peace.

Abu had been working for him since 1980. When the Israeli man was blessed with the birth of a son, Nathan, Abu, ecstatic over his friend's good fortune, brought sweet cakes and a variety of delicious and colourful Palestinian dishes to his friend in celebration of the birth. Abu treated this child as one of his own. He took care of him, played with him, and looked after the boy when he was sick. Nathan became attached to Abu, asking about him every Shabbat. They loved one another. Abu believed that nothing could possibly come between them; he was sadly mistaken.

In the late 1980s, the Intifada began, preventing Abu from crossing the Green Line. Even after 1992, the conclusion of the Intifada, Abu was still prohibited from crossing. It remained this way until well after the start of the second Intifada in the year 2000.

The Israeli man truly missed his friend, Abu. He did not know whether he was alive or dead, as many had perished, both Israelis and Palestinians. Determined to find out, he contacted the media in his desire to discover what had happened to him. If he were alive, he wanted to renew their lost friendship and invite him back to his home.

The media managed to locate Abu Mazen, who was alive and well. He was ecstatic; he had been successful! Abu also had wished to rekindle their remarkable relationship; he missed Nathan as a father misses an absent son, but had lacked the means to do so. Both men could not have been happier when Israeli authorities gave permission for Abu to visit—a precious one-day pass.

This, of course, would not be just an ordinary visit; the television media would be present. It was going to be televised, a "live" event; they both recognized the importance and significance of this meeting, with its implications for the peace process.

Under the media's intense scrutiny, Abu and his Israeli friend met at the Israeli's house. They could not believe that this long-dreamt-about day had arrived! Tears of immense joy and relief swept over them! Despite being surrounded by those intrusive cameras, their lights a glaring reminder of the conflict in which two peoples claimed the same land, they cocooned themselves in their love for one another. The question: "Why could this tender moment not be a private one to be savoured by the two of us?" did not enter their consciousness. They both understood this was the price they had to pay for that most important one-day pass.

"Where is Nathan?" Abu wanted to know. "How is he, my little baby friend?" The father's face lit up with a broad smile, as a man, an Israeli soldier, entered the room and stood at attention directly in front of Abu.

"This is Nathan," the Israeli declared. "Nathan, this is Abu Mazen." At that moment, Abu, who had stood up wanting to hug Nathan, was unable to move; he was paralyzed by his conflicting emotions. He stared at the hated uniform worn by the young man in front of him, a symbol of the Occupation.

Nathan also stood motionless, a blank expression on his face, also experiencing a myriad of emotions. He knew that this man had loved him like a son; he was dazed and confused. Many questions flooded his mind, the foremost being, "Does Abu now consider me to be his enemy? How am I supposed to feel about this man who has provided me with so many of my treasured childhood memories?" With tears in his eyes, unable to endure the scrutiny of the cameras,

Toppling Barriers

he turned around and quickly left the room. Watching his dear friend, the Israeli realized how old Abu suddenly looked; he had aged ten years in a matter of seconds.

Abu was devastated. He had been unable to show Nathan the unconditional love he held in his heart for him. Nevertheless, Abu turned to his friend and told him he should be proud of his son, Nathan.

Nathan's father, aware of Abu's discomfort, told him to forget about it. "This conflict may drive friends and families apart, but not this family, and especially not the two of us," he told Abu. They spent the rest of the day reminiscing, enjoying each other's company, thankful that they had reconnected and were reaffirming their love for one another. Reluctantly, Abu had to leave. His day pass was up. As he went out the door the Israeli gave him a cell phone. They would now stay in contact on a daily basis.

The recollection of friendships like that of Abu and his Israeli friend, combined with the will to have a normal existence and the anger of mothers, could very well topple all barriers to peace.

Raouf Omar

A Journey from Hell

I will never forget the summer of 1982. I was thirty years old and I didn't know whether I would reach the age of thirty-one!

It was the month of June, hot, smoggy, suffocating, and terrifying. I was in Beirut. No longer one of the jewels of the Middle East, it was a city under siege, devastated by war. Sandwiched between the Israelis' relentless military bombardment on one side and the Christian Phalanges on the other, I was in constant fear for my life. The air was filled with the rank smell of putrid garbage, piled high and overflowing; and the accompanying drone of swirling masses of millions of voracious, bloodsucking mosquitoes. The distinctive smell of gunpowder assaulted my senses. Not only was I alone, I also had no food and was starving. My diet consisted of a small supply of water, far more precious than any oil, and a plentiful supply of cigarettes and Scotch. Here, I had discovered what hell might be like!

The surrounding buildings were vacant, lifeless shells. Doors and windows were absent, just like their former inhabitants—those who had been fortunate enough to flee. Bullets and incessant bombing were my reality. I often stayed in hiding, wondering when a fatal projectile would discover my location and blast its way into my body. G-d didn't exist. Life and death had become equals, a single flat line. At that moment, my future had ceased to exist, while the past became a most desirable, yet unattainable, memory in my mind. The cigarettes, Scotch, and these memories were my balm. I knew death could happen at any moment. I was calm and accepting. I could no longer feel fear; I was numb. My days were repetitive. The sound of shelling never stopped; the stench and the mosquitoes' attacks were constant. Scotch was my welcome escape.

My wife, mercifully, was safe in Canada. She was Palestinian, but her family had moved to Canada when she was three years old.

She was a Canadian citizen and was working tirelessly trying to get the Canadian government to issue me a visa; previous applications had been denied because of lack of documentation from both Israeli and Jordanian authorities.

One morning, at four a.m., I decided I had to escape from my apartment. I could no longer cope. My false sense of calm had evaporated. My nerves were shot. My emotional strength was gone. I had reached the bottom. The incessant noise from the bombardment, coupled with the shells that turned night into daylight, had created a psychological war within me far worse than any threatening bullet. My world was coming to an end. I had to risk a visit to the Canadian embassy in downtown Beirut. In bare feet and oblivious to the pain inflicted by the rubble, I managed to make my way unseen to the embassy, grateful for the skills I had acquired as a child playing hide and seek in the alleyways of Balata. Even more miraculous was the fact that it was open, operating by candlelight. It was a secure cavern. All the other embassies had been abandoned, as the situation was regarded as too dangerous.

I was astounded . . . it was unbelievable! I had been granted a visa! My glorious wife's persistence had paid off. Tears of joy cascaded down my face. Hope swelled in my heart. Life instantly became precious once again; death was no longer predominant in my thoughts. However, in times of war, no one could guarantee a safe exit from Beirut. With my visa secured, I retraced my steps back to my apartment, trying to keep myself invisible, safe.

The next day it snowed paper in Beirut. An Israeli plane was dropping leaflets. "If anyone wants to leave, they will be offered safe exit through the Phalangist checkpoints." This was an extremely dangerous proposition. My choice was clear: I could die from a bomb, hunger, or disease . . . or I could leave and possibly die later.

Luck was on my side. I was able to find a taxi driver willing to take me to Damascus, the Syrian capital. I paid one hundred and fifty Lira, although the ride was normally twenty-five; the additional money was for him to provide food for his family. This left me close to penniless, but it was a cheap price to pay for potential life and freedom. An elderly, distraught couple joined us as I threw my battered bag containing what few valuable possessions I had into the car. With my destiny in the hands of G-d, I started my journey to possible freedom.

As we reached the first Phalangist checkpoint, my body turned to ice. "Stop!" they shouted. They grabbed my bag and my Jordanian passport. I was ordered out of the car and told to sit next to a bullet-scarred wall. My bag carried many pictures of me dressed up in various costumes, remnants of earlier days. If they noticed I had been born in a Palestinian refugee camp it would be all over; this wall would be my final resting place. I was terrified. The thirty minutes I had to wait became a lifetime. A soldier came to me with the pictures. Fear rose in me but then I noticed his face was calm, not angry.

"Are you an actor?" he asked.

Instinctively, I lied: "Yes, I am."

"Why are you leaving Beirut?"

"Well, we were shooting a series here, but the war is pushing us out. We are going to Athens, to complete the series." Surely he would smell the lie. The revealing sweat dribbled down my forehead. Suddenly, he shook my hand, put my bag back in the car but not my passport; he wished me luck.

"You will have your passport at the other checkpoint, when you leave our territory." That is exactly what happened, and I believed I was now safe. How naïve can one be? The worst was yet to come.

We continued our journey, heading towards Tripoli, next to the Syrian border. On the way we passed a bakery. "Stop!" I yelled. After two weeks with no food, I was ravenous. Running into the bakery, I bought a loaf of bread. I ate it rapidly and immediately paid the price, doubling over in excruciating pain for having eaten too quickly. I hobbled back into the taxi. Pain could not interfere: I needed to get to Syria.

We arrived in the Cornish area of Tripoli, near a Syrian checkpoint. I could barely contain myself. I was salivating . . . I could taste freedom . . . no meal could ever compare with that moment. It was then that I realized: ahead of us, too many cars were burning. The sounds of bombing and gunfire assaulted my ears. Islamic and Syrian armed forces were clashing. We reached the cars only to see bodies in those burning cars. I will never forget the horrendous smell of burning flesh. Snipers were first firing at the car tires, then bazookas were being used to blow up the immobilized cars. At that moment, I heard whispering sounds in front of me, like bullets hitting water. Suddenly, a bullet struck the front passenger door right where I was sitting.

A Journey from Hell

"Snipers!" screamed the driver. "Put your heads down!" The car rocketed forward, surging past the burning vehicles! We careened into the Syrian checkpoint. Exhilaration swept through my body. We had made it! Incredulously I was safe, as the Syrians presented no problems for me.

The driver was attempting to remain calm, but I could tell that the journey had taken its toll on his body. His complexion no longer appeared healthy, having taken on a haggard, drawn appearance. He drove towards Damascus, stopping in Hems, an old Syrian city, asking me if I wanted to stop for a drink of coffee at a roadside café. We would then continue to Damascus according to our deal. He disappeared into the café.

After some time, when he did not reappear, I anxiously approached the people in the café, mainly taxi drivers, asking if they had seen my driver. I told them my story and about our deal. Anger overcame them. They agreed to drive me for free if they could not locate him. Shortly later, they found him. He was "reminded" of his obligations to me. Shaken, he reluctantly agreed to continue to Damascus. I do not know what happened to the elderly couple who had been travelling with us; perhaps Hems was their final destination.

In Damascus, I had only enough money for a hotel room. I promptly sold my gold chain and, with the money, bought my ticket to a new life. I was again penniless. I had a three-day-long wait for my flight to Montreal, but I was alive. I was safe, enveloped by a sense of rebirth. Euphoria took control of me. Three days later and starving, I stopped a taxi to take me to the airport. I had no money. Dazed, I told him my story.

"I will drive you for free," the driver said, but I just kept repeating that I would trade my musical cigarette lighter and transistor radio for the fare.

"No," he said. "A guy like you should be treated royally." He took me to the airport, but I insisted on making the trade; he reluctantly agreed.

My excitement mounted as I boarded the plane. I could barely contain myself, knowing that after two stops, one in Jordan and one in New York, I would be safely in the arms of Ayda, my loyal, beautiful, determined wife, whose perseverance had given me the gift of life.

The flights were uneventful. I was in a state of shock. I finally landed in New York City, only to be told that I would have to spend a night in a hotel, as my connecting flight to Montreal was the following day. Even though the airline paid for the hotel, I was confused, tired, and started breaking down. My body and mind were "dead." It was at that moment I saw a man who appeared to be Middle Eastern. I approached him. "Could you tell me where this hotel is and how to get there?"

He smiled broadly. "I am also staying there tonight. Follow me." His words comforted me. I was a human being again.

We started chatting and I told him my story . . . my journey from hell. He began to laugh, a pure, unashamed, and unencumbered laughter. What was so funny?

"You know what? I'm Jewish. I have left my country because I have seen too much of this aimless, hopeless war." All our defenses melted; preconceived notions and prejudices became meaningless. We hugged like long-lost friends. We shared a room; we were brothers. The following day he was heading to Argentina to join his relatives.

For me, wrapped in clean, white sheets, it was the best night's sleep in a long time . . . that is, until a nightmare struck. "Rockets, bombs!" I screamed as I fell out of bed, knocked over the night table, and began running madly around the room. The Israeli jumped out of his bed and tried to calm me down. It was no easy task, as the smell of Javex on the sheets had reminded me of the smell of gunpowder and had triggered the nightmare. His compassion soothed my fears, and I relaxed, allowing myself to be healed through his care.

The night was over and together we went to the airport. Before we separated, he said: "Raouf, please accept this money."

"No, all I need is money to make a telephone call to my wife in Montreal." He stayed with me until I completed my call. We wished each other good luck and parted company. Walking away, we both turned around and faced each other simultaneously, saying: "Maybe we will meet again someday."

There are many days I walk with him.

David Ellis

A Volunteer's Experience

Since I spent some time in the Holy Land volunteering on a kibbutz and also working in the copper mines in the Negev Desert, Raouf and Claude asked me if I would consider contributing a story. Initially, I discounted the idea but, upon reflection, decided to put some thoughts on paper. Just as Claude had met his wife, Betty, on a kibbutz, so had I met a wonderful young lady from Montreal. Raouf had also worked in the same copper mines as I had, and I'm very familiar with the West Bank. We have travelled some of the same paths.

It was late summer, 1971, and hot. Just another day, nothing unusual for the Tel Aviv inhabitants—but for me, it was wonderful. The constant, guaranteed heat was a delicacy to be savoured, as were the city's secrets waiting to be revealed to a curious traveller. Wales was my home, my soul, but the weather . . . Now I relished the prospect of a favourable climate to solidify my skin's recently acquired bronze patina. Lobster-red was my norm, infrequent, but proudly displayed. A testament to a rare British summer!

Earlier that day, I had landed at Lod airport, where my passport had been stamped. I had requested that it not be, as I intended to visit other Middle Eastern countries after leaving Israel. In those days, the authorities had the flexibility of either stamping a separate piece of paper and placing it in your passport, or stamping the passport. That stamp would now deny me entry. Not an auspicious beginning, but, there again, I had been told to leave Cyprus by a local judge . . . however, that's another story! Thank goodness for a student card and five pounds, fifty percent of my total funds. That was the cost of a one-way ticket to Israel. You can only sell your blood so many times in one month!

A Volunteer's Experience

Yes, I was one of those countless numbers of hitchhikers wending their way in an easterly direction. However, I wasn't overly concerned, as I had managed successfully over the previous two months on the road and remained optimistic that this would prove to be a temporary glitch. My first priority was to eat, legally, for free; my second priority was to find somewhere to sleep under the stars. My remaining five pounds were to be used only as a last resort, in an emergency. That is when I heard a voice calling my name. Impossible! I didn't know anyone here.

Two hometown friends were standing opposite me! It was early in the evening, and I was sitting in Dizengoff Circle enjoying the spectacle, the hustle and bustle of daily life. The office I had earlier visited for assigning kibbutz volunteers had closed for the day. My friends were on Kibbutz Affikim and enjoying a day off. I knew they were travelling and had recently returned from India. They generously paid for a meal, and I made plans to visit them on their kibbutz when an opportunity arose. I don't recall where I slept that evening – only that it was secure from any overly officious person or persons who might have interrupted my sleep. The weather was of no concern.

The following morning, I visited the volunteer office and was assigned to a kibbutz. I had no preference, and they filled the needs of any particular kibbutz on a daily basis, according to their requirements. I was given a map of Israel and a bus ticket. I didn't have to hitchhike, an already acquired skill later honed to perfection in order to compete successfully against the military, who were constantly flagging down cars. I was off to Kibbutz Massada.

This is not the Masada on the eastern edge of the Judean Desert, overlooking the Dead Sea, where, in 71/72 CE, approximately 900 Jewish rebels committed suicide, preferring death over surrender to the Roman forces.

The kibbutz was located just south of the Golan Heights and on the border with Jordan. Twice since 1948 it had been bombed flat, and a series of trenches crisscrossed the housing area. The children had just started to live above ground once again, having lived the previous two years in underground shelters. Massada wasn't a particularly safe kibbutz. *Objets d'art* scattered around the kibbutz were made from various pieces of shrapnel, and one of the volunteers had lost his leg when he stepped on an explosive device in one of the banana fields.

I remember his having a wooden prosthesis as well as a bicycle to facilitate his movements.

The kibbutz had a swimming pool, an outdoor cinema, and, most important of all, a bed! A luxury, as I was accustomed to sleeping "rough." Massada's economy was based upon bananas and chickens, although it did have a variety of other fruits and vegetables, but these were for their own consumption. The kibbutz was also home to a unit of paratroopers.

Rivka was in charge of the volunteers, who came from various countries. She was firm and tolerated little in the way of inappropriate behaviour. However, she was more forgiving if you had a strong work ethic, were able to contribute meaningfully to the kibbutz, cope with the work assigned to you, and, of course, get up in the morning – not always an easy feat, given the various distractions associated with the diverse backgrounds and behaviours of the volunteers. Fridays were often expulsion days.

My primary job was working in the banana fields. Some of the bunches weighed nearly as much as I did, but I managed by adopting a modified weightlifting technique to hold them above my head after I had severed them from the trees and to pile them onto the tractor that followed us as we worked our way down the rows. If they were put on the ground, I would be unable to lift many of them. I still have my knife with its curved, razor-sharp, serrated blade.

Even though it was physically demanding work, often beginning before dawn, as it became too hot later in the day to work in the fields, I enjoyed it. To me it was a novel experience, and working alongside the paratroopers was a challenge to be met head-on. Initially, they were reserved, but this quickly disappeared when they knew you were prepared to work hard and did not complain if you had to work late into the afternoon and missed lunch as a result. There was always something left in the dining room for you to eat when the workday was finished, prior to the main evening meal. They would also turn a blind eye to many infractions of the kibbutz's code of conduct.

The fields held many hazards in addition to land mines. Wild boar would often trigger an explosion in the border area, and we just hoped not to come face to face with one, as there was no way we would be able to outrun it if it felt threatened. Neither did I have a machete nor an Uzi, which many of the paratroopers had with them. Then there were the spiders, many quite toxic, hiding in the vegetation. My motto was: "If they don't bother me, I won't bother them." Fortunately, I was able to avoid them. Rats loved to make their homes in the banana bunches. Whenever one encountered a nest, the procedure was to give the bunch a vigorous shake, thereby dislodging the parents, if they were in the nest, and then to place your hand inside to feel for any young, which were then disposed of. Experience had taught me to be cautious, as the rats did not always flee, and it was a harrowing feeling to have them run along your arm as you tried to avoid being bitten. Then there were the snakes, one of which, a viper of some kind, that was extremely venomous. The paratroopers joked that there was an antidote for its bite, but its availability was two hours away, and by then it would be too late. A comforting thought!

Yossi, one of the paratroopers, was always demonstrating his skill with the machete. He loved to use it as a throwing knife and was accurate from a considerable distance, consistently hitting his selected target. His forte was throwing a miniscule banana bunch into the air, withdrawing his machete out of the scabbard attached to his waist, throwing it, and slicing the bunch in half before it reached the ground. He was fast and he practised daily. Frankly, I never really appreciated his skill and regarded him to be somewhat of a show-off. However, those feelings were soon to change.

It happened suddenly, but I remember it vividly. It was a hot afternoon, and I was hungry. I was focused on the food to come rather than on the task at hand and had just pushed a large, heavy, hanging, bunch of bananas upwards, as it made it far easier to sever, when a viper's head appeared by the side of my face. It had been resting alongside the bunch and was about to strike. I was startled and my reflexes were slow, but fortunately, Yossi's were not – his machete flew past my ear and decapitated the snake in the blink of an eye. He kicked the head to one side, casually picked up the machete, wiped the blade, smiled, and went about his business. I can only imagine what might have been. Later that day, I thanked him profusely, but he merely shrugged it off. For him, it was nothing. For me, it was everything . . . and I remain eternally grateful.

Claude Weil

The Discharge Day

It is nine a.m.; I am in civilian clothing and dragging my two military duffle bags on a long, straight walkway in a military base in Tel Aviv. This is where, on the first day of boot camp thirty months ago, they had cut my hair, outside, during a night of running around as drill sergeants yelled orders.

Soldiers who are about to be discharged often symbolically drag their duffle bags on the curb as opposed to carrying them. I followed this tradition. By contrast, it is easy to identify the new recruits, as they still have the soft faces of children. They are eighteen years old; the discharged soldiers are wise and weathered forty-year-olds in the bodies of men mostly aged twenty-one to twenty-five. I was twenty-four.

I observed a stream of new male recruits being led to the equipment stores. They noticed this lone soldier dragging his bags. What were their thoughts? I tried to remember what mine had been. That first night had been like a cyclone, a blur. At least they were starting their military life in the morning. I assumed they would not be combat soldiers. Still, in a day from now, every joint in their bodies would hurt. I felt a wave of compassion for them. They had a tough time ahead of them. Three years is a long time when many young people of the world are starting a job or going to college.

An hour later, I became a reservist and a free man. I had served with honour and conviction. This was a life and two deserts ago . . . and eleven wonderful crews that will be with me for the rest of my days.

Though I was well aware that not a single peace treaty had been achieved, I did take part in Bi'r Hasanah on a mission where, for three days, we removed the detonators from antitank mines. My recollection is that they came from a strip of land along the Suez Canal that had been returned to Egypt as part of the long saga of negotiations. I can still picture the pyramid of greenish mines on the long, wooden tables under a canopy, and my unit working in silence. Our officers were right beside us, always leading by example.

Our captain had jumped a few times on one of those mines to demonstrate that it would take an enormous amount of pressure for it to detonate.

Well, it was over, and, on this beautiful April day of 1978, I decided to celebrate my discharge in Haifa while on my way back to the kibbutz. I went straight down to the port in front of the gorgeous, aquamarine bay facing Akko. I entered an Arab restaurant that served the best mutton in the world. The owner knew me. In fact, five years earlier, I had bought a watch from a street vendor right in front of his restaurant. That watch, with a square blue dial, had served me well during my military service. It had been buried so many times in the sand. I regarded it to be my talisman.

The owner made a point of treating me well. He radiated a jovial kindness mixed with good business skills. For him, I was just a young man freshly discharged and facing an unknown future.

Uncertainty is such a common dish in the Holy Land, battered by a long-standing conflict. Palestinians and Israelis share that dish daily.

Israeli soldiers also have to defend the borders of the young state, although by 1981, peace was achieved with Egypt and, later, with Jordan. The vast Sinai I had served in with my unit was Egyptian again. The Bedouins had seen it all. That desert would be an escape for my soul for years to come. It could be a sensual woman dancing under a red sun or a death trap where one could lose his way in a horrific sandstorm. But it had been many times a battlefield for thousands of years.

As I arrived at the bus station, an Arab street vendor wanted my business. I kindly refused, as I did not need any jewellery, but, as I had time on my hands and he had no client, I asked him how business was. "Not so good today, but I also run a small shop with my brother." He was a smart and hard-working man, maybe forty years old.

To this, I replied: "Do you have children?"

"I have six; one of my sons is turning twelve today. He wants me to bring him back a leather belt, like a cowboy."

I also had a child, but now far away in France with Betty. On an impulse, I said, "Listen, my son and my wife are in Europe and I am celebrating my discharge. Can I get a gift for your son since I cannot

The Discharge Day

give one to mine on my discharge day?" He was surprised and said nothing. I walked away. I needed to give, to share my joy.

The old bus station and its surroundings were full of mobile little stores and kiosks. It took me fifteen minutes to find the belt. When I came back, he would not accept the gift unless I'd pick a piece of jewellery. So we traded gifts. He just had taught me a valuable lesson on how to give and receive. We both wore broad smiles and wished each other good health. It was time for me to go.

As I sat in the bus on the way north to the kibbutz, a female air force soldier took the seat opposite to mine. I found out that she was serving near our village. She noticed my military haircut. It is difficult to become a civilian . . .

"Which service are you in?" she asked.

"I am a tanker from the Nahal,[11] now a reservist, as I was just discharged today."

She became curious about my future: "What will you do now; go to university?"

"Yes, I will."

"Do you have a girlfriend?"

I flashed my ring, explained that I was married and a father.

"I have a boyfriend—I think," she replied with a preoccupied look. She had just started her two-year military service. I knew the cluster of buildings she served in was a pretty sad place, bitten by the high winds.

She would not be on a university campus holding her boyfriend's hand. Intuitively I knew, from the seriousness of her lovely face and her dignified posture, that she would serve with dedication. I closed my eyes for a moment, and then looked at the passing fields. Palestinians and Israelis are so beautiful and creative, this land so mesmerizing. Both are worthy of being treated with love and care; both are worthy of the sweetness of peace.

We, and countless others, Jews and Arabs, were immersed in the conflict, but it had no part in my conversation with this young soldier; it was like a sickness you wanted to keep away. We were young and wanted to live a full life.

---

11 The Nahal is an Israel Defence Forces Brigade—Fighting Pioneer Youth.

All of us in the Holy Land wanted to live a full life. Raouf and I have witnessed so many acts of kindness when the souls of people are allowed to expand, to be generous and compassionate.

May peace bless this land and its two peoples. May anger be replaced by their natural good nature and creativity.

On that day, outside the bus windows, the flourishing hills of Galilee, dotted with hundred-year-old olive trees, were a celebration of life.

Somewhere in Haifa, a little Palestinian boy was celebrating his birthday with a real cowboy belt.

Raouf Omar

Spiritual Flashback

The year was 1985, and I was sitting in the living room of my house in Ottawa, Canada. I had fled a war-torn country to build a future in a peaceful country, one filled with hope and generosity. I had run away from violence, looking for an opportunity to establish a good life, indulge in my passion, art, and to show my talent. After only three years of being in Canada, I had managed, working day and night, to save enough money to buy my own home.

It was about three p.m., and I was working on some graphic art designs while my two-and-a-half-year-old daughter was racing around me in her baby walker. My wife was doing laundry in the basement, and all seemed well. As I was fully concentrating on my art, I was not paying attention to my baby daughter as she was pushing the walker towards the stairs leading to the basement. She wanted to see her mother. I became aware of the situation when I heard her strike the top stair of the basement steps. I leapt out of my chair but I was too late; down she went, cartwheeling, smacking her head on the basement's concrete floor.

I was beside her in a split second. She was silent, motionless, and covered in blood. My wife fainted as I picked my daughter up and held her in my arms. Her eyes were wide open and her bottom gum was hanging down, bleeding heavily. I dialed 911, as I feared the worst, but realized she was still alive when she suddenly began screaming.

My wife, who had come out of her fainting spell, was scared to death. We went in the ambulance to the emergency department of the local hospital. The attending doctor told us my daughter needed the services of a specialized dental surgeon to deal with her bottom teeth and gum. The specialist came later that night to operate on her while I held her arms gently to prevent her from moving. The ninety minutes of surgery was difficult for both the surgeon and me, as she continued to scream. My tears covered her. He was successful in putting everything back together, and we were extremely grateful for his skill.

On the way home, I began to shake. The copious amounts of blood and the screaming had brought back all the images I had seen and suffered throughout my ordeal in Beirut, besieged by the Israelis. That night I couldn't sleep because these images were haunting me and memories came flooding back.

In 1982, when I first arrived in Canada, I began to experience severe nightmares, as I was suffering from post-traumatic stress. It was only later that I realized this. I was afraid to go to sleep. Images of dead bodies, the smell of gunpowder and rotting garbage, and the incessant screaming of incoming shells was overwhelming. In Beirut it wasn't as much of a problem, as the smell of Scotch and the taste of cigarettes, which were in my mouth twenty-four hours a day, helped mask the city's rank odours. It took me over a year to escape from these nightmares, but the image of my bloodied daughter had brought them back.

Two weeks after my daughter's accident, I tried to return to my artwork. My hands began to tremble and then started to shake. I felt responsible for her falling down those stairs. I had been too focused on my art and not on her. I had been brought up with the emphasis that family is everything. All that I had previously experienced in my life would be to no avail if I were unable to give her the attention she deserved. I was engulfed in guilt. I decided that had to change, and in reaction to my guilt, I put all my art materials in the garbage. I promised myself that until my children were older, I would not return to my art.

From that moment on, I concentrated on my family; I established a successful restaurant, specializing in Middle Eastern cuisine. It was frequented by a very diverse, multicultural group of people, including both Palestinians and Jews. However, I was dissatisfied despite my success. Deep within me, my desire to pursue art was still there. If I didn't let it out, I knew it would eventually destroy me.

Nineteen ninety-eight marked the beginning of my artistic rebirth. I renewed my love of art, with the support of my customers, many of whom had become my friends. They always talked with me about my paintings, which were visible in the restaurant. I often worked on them in between busy periods. Their appreciation and admiration of the images, inspired by the Holy Land, encouraged me to continue. Among these was a Jewish couple who regularly ate at my restaurant. I considered them to be good friends; they always expressed support and a strong interest in my artwork. However, it was his wife's intervention that was instrumental in freeing my soul and finally erasing those dark, terrifying images from my past.

An artist herself, she delighted in the vibrant colours and images in my art. One day she told me to contact CTV Ottawa, a local television broadcasting company, as they carried a weekly program called *Regional Contact*, which focused on and publicized local artisans. "Your art should be shown all over the country," she said. She followed up by contacting them herself. One week later, CTV was in touch with me. They conducted a televised interview at my restaurant, where much of my artwork is displayed on the walls.

Today, my art is spreading far and wide: nationwide across Canada, and also to Europe, the United States, and the Middle East. I have managed to combine my family life, restaurant business, and passion for art while still maintaining a sense of harmony. Many people ask different questions about my art and some often say: "You are very lucky!" To this I commonly reply: "It's not luck; it is a combination of hard work, focus, and a reflection of the physical and spiritual demands I have experienced."

A Jewish artist displayed compassion and generosity towards me, in Ottawa, just as other Jews had in the Holy Land.

Spiritual Flashback

Appendix

Historical Background

The reader may want to consult the following book: *The Israel-Arab Reader: A Documentary History of the Middle East Conflict* (2008) by Walter Laqueur and Barry Rubin.

This synopsis has been taken directly from the Internet from Wikipedia, which specifically states, not surprisingly:

"The neutrality and factual accuracy of this article are disputed."

For the balance of this detailed article refer to:

Whttp://en.wikipedia.org/wiki/Arab-Israeli_conflict.

"The Arab-Israeli conflict spans roughly one century of political tensions and open hostilities. It involves the establishment of the Zionist movement and the creation of the modern State of Israel in territory regarded by the Pan-Arab and Pan-Islamic movements as Arab Muslim territory and by the Jewish people as their historic homeland.

"The conflict, which started as a political conflict over territorial ambitions following the decimation of the Ottoman Empire, has shifted over the years from the large-scale Arab-Israeli conflict to a more regional Israeli-Palestinian conflict, though the Arab world and Muslim world remain hostile to the Israeli state.

"Despite involving a relatively small land area, the conflict has been the focus of worldwide media and diplomatic attention for decades. Many countries, individuals, and non-governmental organizations elsewhere in the world feel involved in this conflict for reasons such as religious and cultural ties with Islam, Arab culture, Christianity, Judaism, or Jewish culture; or for ideological, human rights, strategic, or financial reasons; or because they are consistently exposed to the conflict by the media.

"Some consider the Arab-Israeli conflict a part of a wider clash of civilizations between the Western world and the Arab or Muslim world. Others claim that the religious aspect is a relatively new matter in this conflict. This conflict has engendered animosities igniting numerous attacks on and by people of opposing sides in countries throughout the world."